MW00769776

more YOUTHWALK

Other Books in This Series

more YOUTHWALK

Bruce H. Wilkinson
Executive Editor

Len Woods
Editor

Paula A. Kirk
General Editor

Walk Thru the Bible Ministries
Atlanta, Georgia

Zondervan Publishing House
Grand Rapids, Michigan

More Youthwalk
Copyright © 1992 by Walk Thru the Bible Ministries
All rights reserved

Published by Zondervan Publishing House

Requests for information should be addressed to:
Walk Thru the Bible Ministries   or   Zondervan Publishing House
4201 North Peachtree Road   Grand Rapids, MI 49530
Atlanta, GA 30341–1362

Library of Congress Cataloging-in-Publication Data

More Youthwalk: faith, dating, friendship, and other topics for teen
survival/ Walk Thru the Bible Ministries, Atlanta, Georgia
    p. cm.
    Summary: Another collection of daily devotional readings to help
young people deal with common problems and concerns
    ISBN 0-310-54591-9 (pbk.)
    1. Teenagers—Prayer-books and devotions—English. [1. Prayer books
and devotions]. I. Walk Thru the Bible (Educational Ministry)
II. Youthwalk.
BV4850.M666   1992   92—8297
242'.63—dc20   CIP
                                                        AC

Cover and interior design by Michelle Beeman
Cover photo by Kevin Johnson
Illustrations by James Wheless, Lewis A. Wallace, and Dan Nelson

Printed in the United States of America

92 93 94 95 / DH / 10 9 8 7 6 5 4 3 2 1

Dedication

When Christ gathered His disciples on the eve of His own greatest hour of testing, He revealed two great characteristics that He desired from His followers—servanthood and fruitfulness. With a rare blend, Nancy DeMoss is an outstanding example of a person who serves the Lord with deep commitment to bearing fruit that lasts for eternity. Nancy DeMoss and her like-minded family have borne much fruit, fruit that has remained. Yet they have done so as servants, hardly noticed, and sometimes not even known by those who are the beneficiaries. With great appreciation for her commitment, wisdom, and single-minded dedication to the cause of Christ, we lovingly dedicate *More Youthwalk* to Nancy DeMoss.

Bruce H. Wilkinson

Acknowledgments

More Youthwalk: Faith, Dating, Friendship, and Other Topics for Teen Survival is the second compilation of topical studies from *Youthwalk,* a magazine for teens published monthly by Walk Thru the Bible Ministries. We thank the many folks who have helped us out over the years, especially all the teens and youth leaders, and even parents who made up our focus groups, posed for photos, and wrote articles and letters that kept us on track. And we're especially grateful to all the people in Walk Thru the Bible's Specialized Publishing Group, from the leadership team to the staff in production.

Special thanks go to Michelle Beeman, Kyle Henderson, Helen Ryser, Robyn Holmes, and Kevin Johnson, our *Youthwalk* design and production team. Also the creative contributions of Gene DiPaolo and Cary McNeal are much appreciated. All have invested their time and talents to produce a book that will make a lasting difference in the lives of young people.

Introduction

As a Christian teenager, are you sometimes confused by the modern world? Do you ever feel pressure to do things you know you shouldn't? Have you ever been asked a tough question about Christianity—and not known the answer? Are you ever embarrassed about sharing your faith?

If you answered any of those questions with a yes, I've got good news for you: You're not alone. But the book you have in your hand can help!

More Youthwalk is carefully designed to help you understand the Bible and apply its truth to your life. *More Youthwalk* will help you establish the Bible as your rock—your sure foundation in this unsure world. No longer will you see the Bible as a book of boring stories about things that happened eons ago. Instead, you'll see the Bible as *relevant*—a vital resource for you to live a happy, successful, and productive life.

We at Walk Thru the Bible Ministries are thrilled to join with Zondervan Publishing House to make this Bible-reading guide available to you.

Bruce H. Wilkinson
President and Executive Editor
Walk Thru the Bible Ministries

How to Get the Most Out of *More Youthwalk*

More Youthwalk is arranged by topics—one for each week. You can start with the first topic or just jump in at any point in the book. Just put a check in the accompanying box to keep your place.

Each topic has an introductory page (to preview the topic) and five devotional pages (one for each weekday—Monday through Friday). Each of the daily devotional pages includes the following five sections:

1. *The Opening Story*—sets up the problem

2. *Look It Up*—shows what the Bible says about the problem

3. *Think It Through*—stimulates your thinking about the problem

4. *Work It Out*—gives practical suggestions for solving the problem

5. *Nail It Down*—shares other passages where you can find more wise counsel about the problem

But that's not all! In addition to the weekly devotional topics, *More Youthwalk* will educate, stimulate, and motivate you with these exciting features:

- *Hot Topic*—Each "Hot Topic" gives biblical answers to an important current issue.

- *Search for Satisfaction*—These pages are stories of humankind's ultimate search: a relationship with God through Jesus Christ.

- *Wide World of the Word*—These fun-filled pages are full of little-known facts about God's Word. Who said learning can't be enjoyable?

- *What on Earth Is God Like?*—These pages present the attributes of God in a down-to-earth way.

Do you want to do great things for God? Of course you do, or you wouldn't be reading this book. Follow the above instructions, and six months from now, you'll know God's Word better than you do today.

And that will be a great thing!

Walk Thru the Bible Ministries

Walk Thru the Bible Ministries (WTB) unofficially began in the early 1970s in Portland, Oregon, with the teaching of Old and New Testament surveys of the Bible. Dr. Bruce H. Wilkinson was looking for a way to innovatively teach the Word of God so that it would change people's lives.

Dr. Wilkinson officially founded WTB in 1976 as a nonprofit ministry. In 1978 WTB moved to its current home in Atlanta.

From these small beginnings WTB has grown into one of the leading Christian organizations in America with an international ministry extending to 21 countries in 30 languages. International branch offices are located in Australia, Brazil, Great Britain, Singapore, and New Zealand.

By focusing on the central themes of Scripture and their practical application to life, WTB has been able to develop and maintain wide acceptance in denominations and fellowships around the world. In addition, it has carefully initiated strategic ministry alliances with over one hundred Christian organizations and missions of wide diversity and background.

WTB has four major outreach ministries: seminars, publishing, leadership training, and video training.

The call of the Lord has been clear and consistent on Walk Thru the Bible as it strives to help fulfill the Lord's Great Commission. The highest ethics and standards of integrity are carefully practiced as Walk Thru the Bible lives out its commitment to excellence not only in ministry but also in its internal operational policies and procedures. No matter what the ministry, no matter where the ministry, WTB focuses on the Word of God and encourages people of all nations to grow in their knowledge of Him and in their unreserved obedience and service to Him.

CONTENTS

Topics

HOT TOPIC

WIDE WORLD OF THE WORD

THE SEARCH FOR SATISFACTION

WHAT ON IS GOD LIKE?

*** SELF-CONTROL *****
Mastering Your Desires

When faced with temptation, many of us are a little like a two-headed monster. One side wants to stand firm; one side wants to give in.

And if that isn't enough, today's dominant philosophies ("Go for it!" and "If it feels good, do it!") do not really encourage us to get a grip on our desires.

But guess what? Either we choose to use self-control and find freedom . . . or do whatever we want and end up enslaved to our desires.

It's not really much of a choice, is it?

"Like a city whose walls are broken down is a man who lacks self-control" (Proverbs 25:28).

****

The gym at 2:30, Friday afternoon:

Enter Doug and Gene who suddenly notice about a dozen members of the school dance team going through a routine.

Gene (excitedly whispering): "Would you look at Pam Powers! She's unbelievable! I sure wish . . . " [Common decency prevents us from printing the rest of his remarks —eds.]

Doug looks at Pam. Then again. Then a third time. In fact, he can't get his eyes or his mind off her. And, as you might imagine, it's not because he's marveling at the talent God has given her in the art of dance.

Scene one: an unbridled thought life

Look It Up: One of the toughest assignments Christians have is self-control of the mind. How can you make sure your thought life is pleasing to God?

• "Set your minds on things above, not on earthly things" (Colossians 3:2).

• "Finally, brothers, whatever is true, whatever is noble, whatever is right, whatever is pure, whatever is lovely, whatever is admirable—if anything is excellent or praiseworthy—think about such things" (Philippians 4:8).

In short, self-control of the mind doesn't come about by magic. It happens when we deliberately choose moment by moment to fill our minds with pure, godly thoughts and not with impure, godless ones.

Think It Through: The human mind is an incredible creation. It's there that we reason, think, predict, use stored information, decide, analyze, believe, and develop attitudes. And, of course, how we think determines how we live—our behavior.

No wonder God's Word is so insistent that we "renew our minds" (Romans 12:2; Ephesians 4:23)

Our ability to live for God directly depends on the way we use our minds.

Work It Out: Guys, when you are tempted to sin, look away! Given our neo-pagan, sex-starved culture, that's a tall order. But God's law is a tall standard.

Girls, the temptations in your thought life are different. You're less likely to lust, more likely to fantasize. Be careful! Too much fantasy can be just as unhealthy.

Here's a guarantee: Spend time every day reading, memorizing, and studying God's Word, and you'll have more control over your thought life.

Nail It Down: Read Psalm 10:4.

******* ONE SELF-CONTROL

Friday, 3:35 P.M. in the parking lot after school:

Suzanne: "Can you believe Heidi? I mean, did you see her coming on to Doug at lunch?"

Christine: "I know, I can't stand her! She's such a tease."

Suzanne: "What do you mean, 'tease?' She's trash! She's been with just about the whole football team."

Christine (shocked): "Has she really?"

Suzanne: "Oh come on, Chris! Everybody knows that! Where have you been?"

Scene two: an uncontrolled tongue

Look It Up: The tongue can be a lethal weapon! So often we use it to gossip, curse, complain, criticize, lie, ridicule, or insult. But, as usual, God has some better ideas for this muscle He created:

• "Reckless words pierce like a sword, but the tongue of the wise brings healing" (Proverbs 12:18).

• "An anxious heart weighs a man down, but a kind word cheers him up" (Proverbs 12:25).

• "Do not let any unwholesome talk come out of your mouths, but only what is helpful for building others up according to their needs, that it may benefit those who listen" (Ephesians 4:29).

Think It Through: Have you ever had the foolish feeling, "Why did I say that?" Have you ever been in a heated argument, said something really cruel, and immediately thought, "Uh-Oh. I'm in trouble now"?

As with anything in the Christian life, verbal self-control isn't something we master in a minute. It takes practice. Self-control is the result of a big decision—following Jesus in general—applied to numerous little decisions—following Him in each specific situation.

Work It Out: Make this your prayer today: "God, I run my mouth way too much and say a lot of things I shouldn't. I want to use my mouth to help others, not to rip them apart.Take control of my tongue. Remind me to speak only at appropriate times and only in appropriate ways."

Then go out and find a friend who's having a bad day. Tell them why you appreciate them. A genuine compliment goes a long way toward building up and benefiting someone who is listening to you.

Nail It Down: Read Proverbs 21:23.

Pray About It:

****** TWO

3

At the Macklin residence tempers are flaring.

Kirk (his voice rising): "I'm not telling you again—get off the phone!"

Donna: "Shut up, Kirk! I'll be off in a minute."

Kirk (yelling): You just talked to her at school. Can't you live one minute without your stupid friends?"

Donna: "At least I have friends."

Kirk: "Only because they feel sorry for you because Corey dumped you for Melissa!"

Donna (throwing a shoe at Kirk): "You pig! Get out!"

Scene three: an unruly temper

Look It Up: In a world full of bully brothers and sarcastic sisters, it's easy for a minor squabble to turn into a major conflict. Solomon gives us some wisdom for controlling our tempers:

• "Better a patient man than a warrior, a man who controls his temper than one who takes a city" (Proverbs 16:32).

• "Do not make friends with a hot-tempered man, do not associate with one easily angered, or you may learn his ways and get yourself ensnared" (Proverbs 22:24-25).

• "An angry man stirs up dissension, and a hot-tempered one commits many sins" (Proverbs 29:22).

Think It Through: Have you ever been an uninvolved bystander and watched someone completely lose it? Didn't they look silly? By allowing their tempers to get the best of them, they ended up making fools of themselves and embarrassing everyone they were with.

Do you know someone who is quick-tempered? Are you? What situations tend to get you the angriest in the shortest amount of time?

Work It Out: The next time you get in a high-voltage situation (like the one above), call a literal timeout. Go somewhere else for as long as it takes to get a clear head.

When you can be more objective, ask yourself, "Who's in control of my life right now—God? . . . or yours truly?"

Stop. Make sure His Spirit is calling the shots.

Then go back and resolve the problem without ranting and raving, without saying and doing things you'll regret later.

Nail It Down: Read Proverbs 14:17.

********* **THREE** **SELF-CONTROL**

Friday, 11:15 P.M., overlooking Lake Wiley, in a 1988 Mustang:

(There's no dialogue in this scene-just a lot of heavy breathing. And since the car's windows are fogged up, we're unable to describe the action for you. But even if we could see into the car, it wouldn't be in good taste to give a detailed account of what's going on. Let's just say that from here it doesn't look like Doug and Suzanne are discussing yesterday's algebra test!)

Scene four: raging hormones

Look It Up: Having self-control over your sexual desires is difficult. Not impossible by any means, but difficult. Maybe that's why God's Word has so many warnings on this subject. For example:

"Live by the Spirit, and you will not gratify the desires of the sinful nature. . . . The acts of the sinful nature are obvious: sexual immorality, impurity and debauchery. . . . But the fruit of the Spirit is . . . self-control. . . . Those who belong to Christ Jesus have crucified the sinful nature with its passions and desires. Since we live by the Spirit, let us keep in step with the Spirit" (Galatians 5:16-25).

Think It Through: Take your pick. You can either
1. listen to your sinful nature, "go for it" sexually, and end up a slave of your passions; or
2. live according to God's Word and experience the freedom of self-control.

Choice #1 angers God, produces guilt and frustration, and ruins relationships. Choice #2 pleases God, produces character and respect, and strengthens relationships.

Work It Out: Some couples get alone in a dark place, start kissing and caressing each other, and then want to know why things get out of hand. Forget it! Self-control begins by avoiding dangerous situations altogether.

If you're having trouble exercising self-control in your dating life, pray this prayer: "Lord, I've really sinned by getting too physical in my relationships, and I want to come back to what's right. Forgive me and give me your strength so that I can say no to my sinful nature. Give me the wisdom to avoid tempting situations in the future."

Nail It Down: Read 1 Corinthians 6:9-11.

Pray About It:

* * * * * * * FOUR

5

A nice, upper-middle-class home at 4:40 on Saturday afternoon:

Vanessa (to her brother Teddy, as she walks through the family room): "Teddy, you couch potato! All you do is lay there and watch TV."

Teddy: "So, all you do is go in the kitchen and stuff your face."

Vanessa: "At least I have a life."

Teddy: "At least I can fit through the door."

Vanessa: "Why don't you grow up?"

Teddy: "Why don't you shut up?"

Scene five: rampant laziness

Look It Up: We've included the exchange between Teddy and Vanessa because it shows two more ways we often fail at self-control: overeating and wasting time.

Regarding our tendency to over-indulge in life's pleasures, Paul warned, " 'Everything is permissible for me'—but not everything is beneficial. 'Everything is permissible for me'—but I will not be mastered by anything" (1 Corinthians 6:12).

Regarding time management, Paul said, "Be very careful, then, how you live—not as unwise but as wise, making the most of every opportunity, because the days are evil" (Ephesians 5:15-16).

Think It Through: Many people eat when they're not hungry or keep eating when they're already full. Is the real solution a new diet, or is it exercising self-control?

Many teenagers spend several hours each day watching the tube or listening to their stereo. How many spend as much time getting to know God better?

Work It Out: Here are some tips on how to take control:

1. Get together with a friend who's also struggling. Agree to pray together about your problem every day for two weeks. (You'll need God's strength to succeed.)

2. Set specific goals like "I'm not eating between meals" or "I'm only watching one hour of TV each day."

3. Keep each other on track. Call your "control partner" and ask, "Is the TV off? Are you making the most of your time?"

Nail It Down: Read Galatians 5:24. On Saturday, read an amazing story of self-control: Matthew 4:1-10. On Sunday, read another: John 2:13. Look especially at verse 15. If Jesus was out-of-control, do you think He could have taken the time to make a whip?

* * * * * * * FIVE SELF-CONTROL

TOUGH QUESTIONS???
There Are Answers!

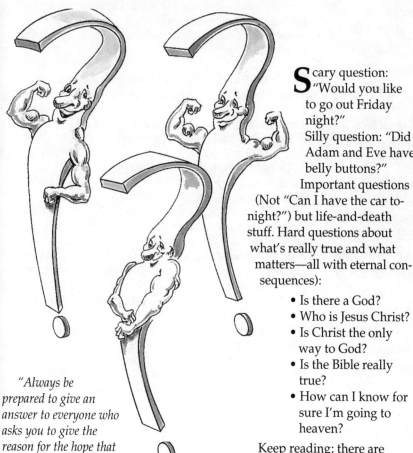

"Always be prepared to give an answer to everyone who asks you to give the reason for the hope that you have" (1 Peter 3:15).

S cary question: "Would you like to go out Friday night?"

Silly question: "Did Adam and Eve have belly buttons?"

Important questions (Not "Can I have the car tonight?") but life-and-death stuff. Hard questions about what's really true and what matters—all with eternal consequences):

- Is there a God?
- Who is Jesus Christ?
- Is Christ the only way to God?
- Is the Bible really true?
- How can I know for sure I'm going to heaven?

Keep reading; there are answers!

???

Most of the students at McKinley High like Mr. Wells, the biology teacher, because he's funny and because it's easy to get him off the subject long enough that he forgets the weekly quiz.

Last Friday someone asked him about God to get him off track.

"God?" he chuckled. "Well, when I was younger I believed in God. But in college, I came to believe that the universe was created by chance and that only physical things—things you can see, hear, touch, taste, and smell—exist."

Seeing God in His creation

Look It Up: We all encounter people in life who think God doesn't exist. God, of course, disagrees.

"The fool says in his heart, 'There is no God' " (Psalm 14:1).

"Since the creation of the world God's invisible qualities—his eternal power and divine nature—have been clearly seen, being understood from what has been made" (Romans 1:20).

Think It Through: There are two fatal flaws in Mr. Wells's belief. First, a chance universe doesn't account for the evidence of intelligent design all around us. The genetic information found in a single cell is like that found in Mr. Wells's biology textbook—highly specified, highly complex.

Does Mr. Wells believe that his textbook had no intelligent designer? Not a chance. Then why does he believe chance can explain the design of the universe?

Second, a strictly physical universe doesn't account for moral laws. You don't doubt that some things are morally wrong—for example, child abuse, murder, and rape. But can you see, hear, or touch the concept wrong? How about the concept right? But if only physical things exist, there is no such thing as right or wrong.

Does Mr. Wells believe torturing infants is as moral as feeding them? Not a chance. Then why does he believe in a universe in which there can be no nonphysical moral laws?

Work It Out: Look at the life all around you. Either you are meaningless—the result of a cosmic accident billions of years ago—or else a good Creator exists and designed you for His good purpose. Take your pick.

Nail It Down: Read Acts 17:22-31.

?????????? ONE TOUGH QUESTIONS

Reid and Jay are hanging out, watching television after school. After watching Geraldo get hit in the head by a flying chair, they flip the channel and find three guys wrapped in white sheets on the Oprah Winfrey talk show.

It turns out all three are gurus from India. Each one claims to be God.

After watching them argue for about five minutes, Reid turns to Jay and smirks, "If any one of those clowns really was God, the world would be in serious trouble."

When the Creator visited this planet

Look It Up: When someone says, "I'm God," we need to check out his credentials. Do his words, character, and behavior support his claim?

Jesus said, "I tell you the truth, . . . before Abraham was born, I am!" (John 8:58). When Jesus said "I am," He was speaking the name of God that no Jew would dare utter and thus claiming to be God. That's why his adversaries "picked up stones to stone him" (verse 59).

Jesus backed up His claim.

• He demonstrated authority over the physical world: He calmed storms (Mark 4:39) and healed various sicknesses (Mark 3:10).

• He exercised authority over the spiritual realm by casting out demons (Luke 4:35).

• He displayed authority over death by raising others (John 11:43-44) as well as Himself (John 2:19).

• He taught that people should worship only God (Matthew 4:10) and then accepted worship (John 20:28)!

Think It Through: We can't say Christ was merely a good man, a great teacher, or an example. There are only two options: Christ was either God or a bad man.

If he was truly a good man, He was God; for good men tell the truth, and He claimed to be God. If He was not God, He was a bad man; for His claim to be God was either a lie or was an insane delusion. And most of us don't consider liars and deluded egomaniacs to be good men.

Work It Out: Thank Christ for being willing to leave the perfection of heaven in order to come to a sinful world and die for you:

Nail It Down: Read Hebrews 1:1-3, 8.

Pray About It:

??????? TWO

A narrow way is better than no way

Claire is amazed when she sees a popular advice column.

It seems a woman has written in to complain that her grown children, who are committed Christians, are trying to persuade her to believe in Jesus Christ. She tells the columnist that she resents their "preaching," but at the same time she wonders if what they say is true.

The columnist replies that all religions worship the same God, and He allows everyone into heaven. She concludes by telling the advice-seeker not to worry, because "there are many ways to God."

Look It Up: A lot of people believe that. Did Jesus?

• "I am the way and the truth and the life. No one comes to the Father except through me" (John 14:6).

• "I am the gate; whoever enters through me will be saved" (John 10:9).

Notice Jesus didn't say that He was only one of many ways or gates. He said, "No one comes to the Father except through me." That's totally exclusive.

When Jesus made those claims, He was either telling the truth, lying, or mistaken. Those are the only options. And considering that Jesus was God in human form, somehow the last two options don't seem very likely.

Think It Through: Imagine everyone in your city is starving. But a gigantic grocery store is giving out free food to anyone who will come inside and receive it.

Would it make sense to stand outside and complain that the store only had one entrance? Can you imagine someone saying, "I want to get inside by going through the roof and they're saying I can't. How unfair can you get!"

So why do people complain about Christ being the only way to God? Better one way than no way!

Work It Out: Are you counting on reaching God by being a good, sincere person? Forget it.

If you've never turned from your sins and trusted Christ alone for salvation, please do so right now!

If you've already trusted Him, ask God for a chance to discuss your beliefs today. A lot of your friends are standing outside the "grocery store" of heaven, starving spiritually. Show them the entrance: Jesus Christ!

Nail It Down: Memorize Acts 4:12.

?????????? THREE TOUGH QUESTIONS

Colleen and Paula are talking to Tom, their youth pastor. He's holding a bunch of books.

"What's all that?" Colleen asks.

"Well, this Sunday we're gonna study about how we know the Bible is really from God. These are all books considered holy by other religions."

Paula is stunned. "You mean some people don't believe the Bible?"

Tom smiles. "Well, the Mormons have The Book of Mormon; Muslims believe in The Koran; Hare Krishnas use a book I can't even pronounce; Christian Scientists read stuff written by Mary Baker Eddy . . ."

The Book is not just any book

Look It Up: With so many groups claiming to have "God's Word," it's nice to know the Bible is trustworthy.

The Old Testament is constantly punctuated by the phrases "this is the word of the Lord" and "then the Lord said."

The New Testament says "all Scripture is God-breathed" (2 Timothy 3:16).

Perhaps the authors of all those more recent books listed by Tom should consider this warning:

"Every word of God is flawless. . . . Do not add to his words, or he will rebuke you and prove you a liar" (Proverbs 30:5-6).

Think It Through: Despite being written by more than 40 authors over a period of about 1,600 years, the Bible displays amazing unity and continuity.

Despite persecution, perversion, criticism, abuse, and time, the Bible has survived virtually intact.

What's more, the Bible is completely accurate with respect to history, archaeology, and prophecy.

Finally, the Bible has had a greater impact on culture, thought, and the lives of individuals than any other book.

What other book can truthfully make such claims?

Work It Out: Since the Bible is really the Word of the living God, then it only makes sense that you ought to learn as much about it as you can. Read and think about the Bible daily, and memorize as much of it as you can.

Establish that habit early in life; later in life, you'll be so glad you did.

Nail It Down: Read Psalm 119:105.

Pray About It:

??????? FOUR

11

One day while staying after school to work on their term papers, Debbie and Gil got into a conversation about church. That led to a serious discussion about Christianity (not a typical conversation in the library).

"Look, I don't understand everything about it . . . I just know when I die, I'm going to heaven," Debbie finally said.

Gil couldn't believe it. "How can you be so sure?"

"You can't really know about all that until after you die. I mean, I try to live a pretty decent life. I think I'm an okay person. But I'm sure not gonna act like heaven's a definite thing!"

How to know where you'll go

Look It Up: You may be surprised at how many people think like Gil. They believe that when you die, God takes all your good works and bad works and dumps 'em on a huge, cosmic scale. If the good outweighs the bad, you're in. If the opposite is true well . . .

When it comes to something so important, God doesn't want us to be in the dark. He spells it right out so there's no guesswork.

"God has given us eternal life, and this life is in his Son. He who has the Son has life; he who does not have the Son of God does not have life. . . . I write these things to you who believe in the name of the Son of God so that you may know that you have eternal life" (1 John 5:11-13).

Think It Through: It boils down to this: If you "have the Son," you have eternal life and are headed for heaven. To say you "have the Son" is just another way of saying you believe in Jesus. You trust Him (and Him alone) to forgive your sins and make you right with God.

Work It Out: Maybe for a class in sociology, or history your teacher would let you conduct a survey on "Religious Beliefs of Students at _____ High School." One of the questions might be: "Assuming you believe in God and in a real place called heaven, how does one get to heaven?"

Not only would this help you find out what your friends believe, but you might also get an opportunity to share with some of them what the Bible says on the subject.

Nail It Down: Read John 5:24. On Saturday read Paul's answer to some tough questions: Romans 9:19-21. On Sunday read Solomon's answer: Ecclesiastes 12: 13-14.

?????????? FIVE **TOUGH QUESTIONS**

KNOWING GOD
Who in the World Is He?

Who is God? The man upstairs? A force? A tyrant? A cosmic Santa Claus? This week become a theologian (one who studies about God) and join us as we check out what God is *really* like. You might be surprised. You might even be shocked. But one thing is sure: your relationship with Him will never be the same!

"Let not the wise man boast of his wisdom or the strong man boast of his strength or the rich man boast of his riches, but let him who boasts boast about this: that he understands and knows me, that I am the LORD" (Jeremiah 9:23-24).

Ellen feels frustrated. All her life she's heard about God. In her Bible she's read about God. She and her Christian friends talk about God. Ellen believes in God, and seven years ago she became a child of God by trusting Christ as her Savior. So why the frustation, Ellen?

"I don't know. It's just that sometimes I wish I could actually see God. Or when I feel really down, have Him reach out and give me a big hug. Wouldn't it be great to have Him right there with you all the time? Wow! Then you'd never doubt again!"

Understanding God's touch

Look It Up: Ever feel like Ellen? Most of us do at one time or another. Our skeptical society usually dismisses whatever can't be perceived with the senses. This attitude even affects Christians, making us doubt. The frustration comes because God can't be known on those terms.

Why? Because "God is spirit" (John 4:24).

What does that mean? It means He is, by nature, invisible. He doesn't have a material body like we do. And since He's not confined to a body in a specific location, He can be everywhere at once! He is right there with Ellen wherever she is, and at the same time He is with you and me!

Think It Through: If God doesn't have a physical body, why do some Bible verses mention His "ears" (1 Peter 3:12) or His "hands" (Psalm 19:1)? Such passages don't mean that God literally has a body. Those are figures of speech intended to show that God, though Spirit, can do those acts that require body parts in a man. The examples just given mean that God can hear our prayers and help us in our time of need.

Yes, sometimes the Bible records instances in which men "saw" God (Exodus 24:10; Genesis 18:1; Isaiah 6:1). But these individuals saw manifestations of God, not His invisible essence (John 1:18).

Work It Out: Thank God that, because He is spirit—not limited to a material body, He can be everywhere at once. Thank Him for being with you right this very minute. As you go through the day, remember you are always in His presence.

The next step? Live like it!

Nail It Down: Read John 1:1-18.

✝ ✝ ✝ ✝ ✝ ✝ ✝ ONE **KNOWING GOD**

Brent is the kind of guy who's always "up."

Today, however, Brent is depressed. In science class he saw a movie about what might happen if there were a nuclear war. At church this evening he heard a visiting missionary talk about the billions of people in hundreds of countries around the world who are lost without Christ. Suddenly, Brent feels overwhelmed —very small, very insignificant, and very powerless. What can he possibly do to make a difference in such a desperate and dying world?

A big God = small problems

Look It Up: Isaiah 40 can help Brent remember the greatness and power of God: "Who has measured the waters in the hollow of his hand, or with the breadth of his hand marked off the heavens?" (v. 12).

In other words, God is so big He could (if He wanted to) "palm" the universe like Michael Jordan palms a basketball!

That's not all: "Surely the nations are like a drop in a bucket; they are regarded as dust on the scales" (v. 15).

Imagine all of Canada and the United States— thousands of miles of plains, deserts, forests, lakes, rivers, mountains, and valleys. Yet God is so big that, to Him, both of these nations are like tiny specks of dust or little drops of water.

Wait, there's more: "He brings princes to naught and reduces the rulers of this world to nothing" (v. 23). God, not world leaders, is ultimately in charge of His world.

Think It Through: If God really is as awesome and powerful as these verses say He is, why do you think we so often get so worried about so many things? Do most Christians treat their majestic and great God as they should? Do you?

Work It Out: List all the things that you feel incapable of doing or facing today. Write across the top of the list, "Glory and power belong to our God" (Revelation 19:1). Across the bottom write, "He gives strength to the weary and increases the power of the weak" (Isaiah 40:29).

We can make a difference in God's world because He gives His power to us.

Nail It Down: Memorize Philippians 4:13.

Pray About It:

✝ ✝ ✝ ✝ ✝ ✝ TWO

Change. Everybody goes through some changes, but Karen feels like she's in a whirlwind. When her family recently moved from Idaho to Alabama she had to break up with her boyfriend, leave all her friends, and kiss her hobby—snow-skiing—good-bye.

Maybe you can identify with her anger: "Everything is always so new and different. Everything's always changing! I hate it! Why do we keep moving every other year? Why can't we just settle down somewhere and be normal?"

Solid Rock in a changing world

Look It Up: Sometimes change is for the better, but sometimes it isn't. In a changing world, where can we find security? Consider these verses describing God:

"I the LORD do not change" (Malachi 3:6).

"The Father of the heavenly lights . . . does not change" (James 1:17).

God is the solid rock we can cling to and count on. Since He's perfect, He can't get better. Since He's perfect, He can't become anything less. His character is completely consistent day after day. The truth of His Word never goes out of style. He does not waver in His plans or purposes. He can't love you any more than He already does, and He'll never love you any less.

What security! What comfort! What a change-less truth for a changing world!

Think It Through: Since everyone feels like Karen sooner or later, spend a couple of minutes thinking about the consistency of God. If God doesn't ever change, what does that say about:
1. His love for you?
2. His attitude toward sin?

Work It Out: Think of the most faithful, dependable person you know. Ask that person to share with you some tips on dependability. Then do at least one thing he or she suggests—today.

God will never, ever change in His nature, His Word, or His dealings with us! He is dependable and sure. Now that's good news!

Nail It Down: Read Hebrews 13:8.

✝ ✝ ✝ ✝ ✝ ✝ ✝ THREE **KNOWING GOD** ✝

God the Father knows best

Andy: "I don't get it. You get to the age—14 or 15—where you start having strong feelings for someone and then your parents quote you the Bible and say, 'Now son, we know you like Leslie a lot but you have to wait till you're married to have a sexual relationship. God's plan is that sex is only for marriage.'

"Hey, I won't get married for another 10 years! That's ridiculous! God doesn't really expect that, does He?"

Look it Up: The real issue here isn't sex—it's God's wisdom. Wisdom is the unusual ability to understand situations and people and how to deal with them. Does God have such understanding?

"To God belong wisdom and power; counsel and understanding are his" (Job 12:13).

"He made the earth by his power; he founded the world by his wisdom and stretched out the heavens by his understanding" (Jeremiah 51:15).

Hundreds of verses repeat this truth: God created the universe; therefore He knows what He's talking about.

Think It Through: Every new VCR comes with an owner's manual. This booklet describes how the VCR is put together, how to hook it up, how to use it, and what to do if you have problems. Most people don't read their manual. They bury it in some drawer and then wonder six months later why their VCR keeps eating their tapes!

We sometimes do the same thing with God. Having made us, He knows what's best for us and how we can have the most satisfying life possible. He's provided an "owner's manual" for us—the Bible—so that we can maximize our performance for Him. But if we ignore His wisdom, we can end up like a trashed videotape.

Work It Out: On one side of a sheet of paper write: "God—100% wisdom (Job 12:13)" This represents God's total wisdom in every area of life. On the other side write your name and an estimate of how much of all the wisdom in the world you possess. Rejoice that you serve a wise God who is willing to share His wisdom with His unwise children (Ephesians 1:17).

Nail It Down: Read James 1:5.

Pray About It:

FOUR

✝ ✝ ✝ ✝ ✝ ✝

One thing really bothers P. J.

"I know God is all powerful—just look at all the miracles in the Old Testament, or the stars and oceans. And I know He is wise; He knows what's best.

"But I . . . well, I guess I'm just afraid God isn't always good. I mean, if God is really as good as people say He is, why does He allow so many incredibly horrible things to happen in the world?"

The truth of God's goodness

Look It Up: According to the Bible, the issue of God's goodness is settled: God is good!

"The LORD is good to all; he has compassion on all he has made" (Psalm 145:9).

How does God show His goodness? "The LORD upholds all those who fall and lifts up all who are bowed down" (v. 14). He opens His hand and satisfies "the desires of every living thing" (v. 16). He is "loving toward all he has made" (v. 17). He is "near to all who call on him" (v. 18). And He "watches over all who love him" (v. 20).

Think It Through: Why then is there evil in the world? Because Adam chose—and people choose—to sin.

Why did God allow Adam to do such a bad thing? Though the answer is ultimately a mystery, some have answered that God was good in creating Adam with a free will—the ability to sin or not to sin. To God, apparently, creating Adam free, but able to sin, was a higher good than creating Adam sinless, but unable to be free.

Think of all the people who drown every year. Suppose we passed laws that no one could swim, ski, surf, fish, sail or go anywhere near any body of water. With such laws we could eliminate most drownings. But the freedom to enjoy the water is a higher good than eliminating all water accidents.

Work It Out: Jot down all the ways God has shown His goodness to you. Include spiritual as well as material blessings. Try to list at least 25 good things. (And then spend some time thanking Him!)

Nail It Down: Memorize Psalm 106:1. On Saturday, read about the ultimate act of goodness: Romans 5:8. On Sunday, memorize that verse too.

✝ ✝ ✝ ✝ ✝ ✝ ✝ FIVE KNOWING GOD ✝

18

GOD by Gabriel

reetings. I'm the Angel Gabriel. You know, the angel who gave the Virgin Mary the news that she was going to have a very special baby—the Son of God.

After all these years I'm still in the news business, but this time I'm doing a feature story.

What's that? Who's my feature about?

Today my subject is God.

First, He gave you humans a written description of Himself. (And no matter how many negative comments I hear about the Bible—"boring," "violent," "complicated," "long," it's still the greatest book in the world.

Next He provided you with an "up close and personal" glimpse of Himself. He literally entered your world. He let you see Him, touch Him, and watch Him work. Jesus of Nazareth was God—God in human skin! (And that still blows my angel mind.)

All that, and yet you'd think He'd never said a word—that He was a mute! Despite it all, some people deny that He even exists. (Man, are they in for a surprise!) Others have

somehow developed all sorts of crazy descriptions and ideas about Him.

For instance, God never called Himself "the man upstairs!" Nor did He ever reveal Himself as "the Force" or "the Universe."

Just answer me this: Have you ever read His Book? Have you ever taken a long, hard look at the life of Jesus, His Son?

Well, since so many of you are either confused or have forgotten, let me remind you who God really is.

He is your
• Creator (Genesis 1:1);
• Shield (Psalm 3:3);
• Fortress (Psalm 18:2);
• Shepherd (Psalm 23:1);
• Owner (Psalm 24:1);
• King (Psalm 47:2).

Best of all, when you get to know God through faith in His Son Jesus Christ, He also becomes your Father (John 8:41).

Today when you think of God, think of Him in those terms, okay? And give thanks to Him for the day long ago when Mary gave birth to His Son.

MANY WAYS TO GOD

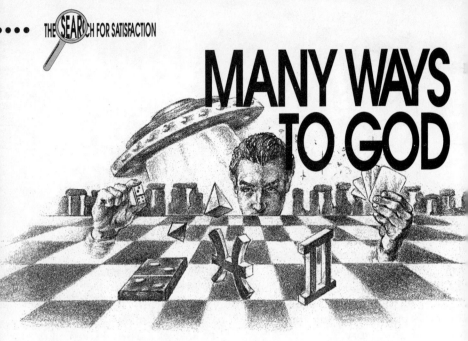

People committed to New Age beliefs and practices would have us believe that we can get in touch with God and become whole individuals through any of the following techniques:

Yoga, transcendental meditation, transchanneling, holistic medicine, rebirthing, REIKI, psychic art, astrology, hypnotherapy, astral projection, past-life therapy, metaphysics, dream analysis, handwriting analysis, floating in isolation tanks, iridology, reflexology, body electronics, positive self-imaging, internal visualization, numerology, past-life regression, psychic readings, Shustah cards, contacting UFO's and extraterrestrials, relaxation techniques, chanting, sandplay therapy, self-hypnosis, EST and/or Forum, biofeedback, levitation, parapsychology, Silva mind control, Tarot card readings, rolfing, martial arts, bioenergetics, crystals, positive self-talk, and T'ai Chi (provided, of course, that you have the bucks to get involved in these often extremely expensive practices!).

Compare all this with what Jesus Christ said:

"I am the way and the truth and the life. No one comes to the Father except through me" (John 14:6).

A simple statement. An exclusive statement. Jesus didn't say He was a way, but *the* way. That means New Age thought is, at best, an expensive mistake; at worst, a horrible pack of lies.

If you haven't trusted Christ, do so right now. Tell Him that you want to be forgiven of your sins, that you want to know God, and that you want to experience the true life that only He can bring. (And don't forget to thank Him that His gift of eternal life is free!)

EVANGELISM
The Great Co-Mission

"Jesus said . . . 'As the Father has sent me, I am sending you'" (John 20:21).

How many times have you heard people make statements like, "Christians have an obligation to tell others about Jesus"?

Probably enough times to make you feel guilty. Probably enough to make you think, "Okay! I get the message! Quit telling me I need to do it and start showing me how!"

That's what the next few pages are all about: giving you some practical tips on how to communicate the best news of all.

(Wouldn't it be great if every reader of this book introduced a friend to the Lord this month?)

E very Sunday it's the same. The minister announces,"Don't forget our evangelism night. We'll meet here at the church for a short time of prayer. Then we'll go out for an evening of witnessing."

David, 16, leans over to his friend Bill and whispers, "Can't he see that no one is interested? I would never go out and do that."

Shawn, 15, cringes at the announcement. She remembers the time an elderly couple went out witnessing and cornered one of her non-Christian friends. That was eight months ago, and the friend still hasn't come back to church.

What witnessing is all about

Look It Up: Try to find even one command for Christians to "go out witnessing" in the Bible. Guess what? You can't! That's because witnessing isn't merely something we go out and do on a predetermined night of the week. To the contrary, witnessing is a lifestyle.

Just before He returned to heaven, Jesus said, "You will receive power when the Holy Spirit comes on you; and you will be my witnesses" (Acts 1:8).

The epistles then describe what it means to be a witness for Him.
- Be like Christ (Romans 8:29).
- Have godly character (Galatians 5:22-23).
- Love your neighbor (Galatians 5:14).
- Be different from the world (Romans 12:2).
- Work hard (Colossians 3:23).

Think It Through: That doesn't mean "going out witnessing" is wrong. When done right, it can be very effective. But realize this: Even when you don't talk about your faith, you are a witness. More than your words, your life reveals who you are and what you believe.

Do people notice anything different about you? Are your non-Christian friends being drawn closer to God because they see Christ in your life?

Work It Out: As promised, we're going to give you some practical pointers this week on exactly how to bring others into the family of God. Today we want to emphasize the fact that evangelism is not just an activity where we talk to people about God (though that's a big part of it). Evangelism is a way of life.

Hmmm. Maybe that's why the super-evangelizing, first-century church was called "the Way" (Acts 9:2).

Nail It Down: Read 1 Peter 2:9-12.

++++++++++ ONE **EVANGELISM**

Jill's method of witnessing? To say nothing. "I just think it's more important to live like a Christian than to always go around talking about it. Besides, I'm not a Bible scholar and I really wouldn't know how to explain all that complex theology stuff."

Don's method of witnessing? To talk about everything— and argue about anything. Yesterday he had a golden opportunity to talk reasonably about the Lord. He ended up in a shouting match with one of his friends about the Pope!

But I don't know what to say!

Look It Up: No matter what Jill says, it is important to witness verbally. It's equally important not to argue about issues that are irrelevant.

Question: So what should Christians talk about when witnessing?

Answer: Mere Christianity. That's what C. S. Lewis called the body of beliefs that all true Christians have always believed. Paul outlines some of those beliefs in a witnessing speech he gave in Athens.

• God is creator of heaven and earth (Acts 17:24).

• God has a law that men have disobeyed (Acts 17:29).

• The Resurrection proves that Christ will judge the world (Acts 17:31).

• Therefore, all people should repent through the Man that God has appointed (Acts 17:31).

Think It Through: Most court cases are settled when witnesses tell what they have personally experienced. On rare occasions experts are brought in to provide testimony that can help the jury.

Think of yourself as an ordinary witness. When sharing the gospel, tell people about your own encounter with Christ. Then, if more evidence is needed, utilize expert witnesses—your youth leader, tapes or books by authors who answer the tough questions.

Work It Out: Remember two things:

First, it's not enough just to witness by your lifestyle. Living a good life is important, but if you never *tell* people why your lifestyle is different, they'll go to hell thinking, "Wow! _____ sure is a nice person."

Second, stick to what C. S. Lewis called "mere Christianity"—the essentials that all true Christians share.

Nail It Down: Read Romans 10:14.

Pray About It: ———————————————

+‑+‑+‑+‑+‑+‑+‑+‑+ T W O

23

Consider two very different scenarios:

• Gene trusted Christ when he was in the ninth grade. What was it that drew him to the Lord? "I met a guy in my art class who was a Christian. He took me with him to a youth group meeting. There I saw about 35 people who really cared about each other. I had never been around a group like that. It made a big impression on me."

• Sonia wasn't a Christian when she started going to a church last summer.

After seeing how the people treated each other there, she still isn't a Christian. "What a bunch of hypocrites!" she exclaims.

The witness of the body

Look It Up: Jesus said, "A new command I give you: Love one another. As I have loved you, so you must love one another. By this all men will know that you are my disciples, if you love one another" (John 13:34-35).

Speaking about this verse, the late Christian philosopher Francis Schaeffer said that unbelievers have every right to doubt our Christianity if we fail to love our fellow Christians. Often our love for each other is what ultimately draws people to Christ.

Think It Through: In a world that's drowning in bitterness and hatred, brotherly love is God's life preserver.

How about your youth group? Your Christian friends? Is division and gossip the norm? Are there lots of little factions and cliques within the big group? If there are, maybe someone like Sonia has left one of your meetings convinced that Christianity is a big joke.

Work It Out: Sometimes you may read this part of the page and say, "That's a good idea, but I just don't have the time." Today you need to make time.

If there are Christians at your school or church that you don't get along with, you need to go to them and get things straight—immediately!

It doesn't matter who is at fault or who started it. Here's what matters:

• God is watching. He cares about all members of the body of Christ (including those you don't like).

• Non-Christians are watching. If we don't love, they have every right to view our claims with skepticism.

Straighten out the problem and begin to love each other as Christ commands. Your witness to unbelievers will be incredible.

Nail It Down: Read John 15:12-13.

++++++++++ THREE EVANGELISM +

Yesterday Melanie saw a depressed-looking woman in a stalled car during rush hour traffic. When Melanie approached the car and tried to talk to the woman about Christ, the woman cursed her.

"Some people are so against the gospel," Melanie moans.

• After his youth group's beach evangelism day, Clint was disappointed. "I talked to five people and never once got all the way through the little booklet. It was a disaster."

Let the Master show you how

Look It Up: For lessons in evangelism, we need to look to Jesus, the Master Evangelist. Note His style:

1. He was sensitive to people. He met their physical and spiritual needs (Mark 6:34-44).

2. He adjusted His approach to meet each situation.

To the woman getting water at Jacob's well, He said, "Everyone who drinks this water will be thirsty again, but whoever drinks the water I give him will never thirst" (John 4:13-14).

To Nicodemus, He spoke of a new birth (John 3:7).

To the Jews who were discussing the Old Testament miracle of manna from heaven (see Exodus 16), He claimed to be the "bread of God . . . who comes down from heaven and gives life to the world" (John 6:33). The basic message was always the same, but Jesus shared it in a way that fit each situation.

Think It Through: What could Melanie have done differently in her witnessing attempt? Suppose Clint had worried less about "getting through" his booklet and concentrated more on really listening to the people he met. Might his experience have been more positive?

Work It Out: Pick out a non-Christian friend or neighbor with whom you've always wanted to share your faith in Christ. Then do three things.

• Begin to pray daily for that person.

• Show love by helping out, doing little things, and lending a hand in any way possible.

• Look for opportunities in your conversations to creatively share what makes you tick . . . the reality of Jesus in your life. (Make sure you let your friend know that Jesus can also be real in his or her life too!)

Nail It Down: Read Acts 8:26-40.

Pray About It:

FOUR

+-+-+-+-+-+-+-+-+

25

Last night Stan and Rudy got into a deep discussion about the Lord. Rudy listened carefully as Stan gave a great explanation of the gospel. Rudy asked about a million questions and one by one, Stan gave intelligent answers. When the conversation ended, Stan asked Rudy if he was ready to trust Christ. Rudy replied, "Nah. Maybe when I'm older."

Stan is still shocked today. "I can't believe it! I answered every one of his objections.

"He understood; he even agreed with my answers. But he still refused to trust Christ. What happened?"

Let the Spirit be your guide

Look It Up: Apart from the power of the Holy Spirit, our evangelism is like trying to raise the dead—hopeless.

The Holy Spirit must be active in our lives. In the Book of Acts, the disciples' ministry was always the result of the Holy Spirit's power working in them.

"And they were all filled with the Holy Spirit and spoke the word of God boldly" (Acts 4:31).

The Holy Spirit must also act in those we wish to win to Christ. Jesus declared, "No one can come to me unless the Father who sent me draws him" (John 6:44).

Think It Through: Bill Bright, founder of Campus Crusade for Christ, has wisely said, "Successful witnessing is simply sharing Christ in the power of the Holy Spirit and leaving the results to God."

In other words, the pressure isn't on us. God is the One who draws people to Himself. Our responsibility is to faithfully live out and proclaim the message of Christ. The rest we leave to God.

Work It Out: Do you want to be a successful witness? Right now ask the Lord to take control of your life. Make sure you're submitting to Him in every area—academics, athletics, dating/social life, finances, family relations.

You may need to confess some areas where you've been disobedient. (If you're hiding some secret sin you won't be completely useful for Him.)

Ask God to fill you with His Spirit (Ephesians 5:18) so you can live and witness effectively. Then go out and combine your walk and your talk!

Nail It Down: Read Romans 8:6-8. On Saturday, compare John 6:44 and John 6:65. On Sunday, read Acts 18:9-10. What was the source of Paul's confidence in evangelism?

+-+-+-+-+-+-+-+ FIVE EVANGELISM

♥♥♥♥♥♥♥ LOVE ♥♥♥♥♥♥♥♥♥
The Real Master's Degree

Would you like to experience the excitement and maturity of being a graduate student—while you're still in high school? You can by enrolling today in Love University.

The next few pages describe the courses offered at Love U. This institution of "higher" learning has been around forever, and those who have earned a Love U. "Master's" degree have gone on to eternal success.

Interested?

C'mon! It can't hurt to at least check it out.

"And so we know and rely on the love God has for us. God is love. Whoever lives in love lives in God, and God in him" (1 John 4:16).

♥♥♥♥♥♥♥♥♥♥♥♥♥♥♥♥♥♥♥♥♥♥♥♥♥

Meet Randy Crowell, 17, who has one year of high school left.

Randy plans to go to the University of Florida next fall and major in accounting. He says it's because accountants make a lot of money. But the truth (and maybe he doesn't even realize it) is that he's trying to earn approval from his workaholic father (who's an accountant for a big firm).

Randy's pretty normal. He just wants to be loved and accepted. The best way for him to find what he's looking for would be for him to go to Love U. and sit in on course 101: The Source of Love.

Course 101: The source of love

Look It Up: It's not wrong to want to be loved and accepted. The problem comes when we go looking for love in the wrong places. We need to go right to the source—the God of the universe. Why?

• His very nature is love: "God is love" (1 John 4:16).

• His love never stops. (Note that the phrase "His love endures forever" occurs 26 times in Psalm 136!)

• He alone is able to give us the ability to love: "But the fruit of the Spirit is love" (Galatians 5:22).

Think It Through: Imagine this scenario: You're lost in a hot, dry desert. You encounter some other wanderers sitting around a dusty riverbed trying to quench their thirst with a tiny trickle of water. A man comes over a dune and shouts, "Hey, if you'll follow that trickle a few miles east, you'll find a giant spring of refreshing cool water!"

Which would make more sense: to settle for a few drops, or to go to the source and have all the water you could ever want?

Work It Out: No human love—from parents, family, or friends—can ever completely satisfy our deepest needs. Only God's love is perfect and able to truly meet our needs. That's the first lesson to learn at Love U.

Assignment Time: If you're feeling unloved just now, splash around in these verses for a few minutes: Romans 8:35-39; Ephesians 3:17-19; 1 John 4:7-21.

When it comes to love, there's no one like the God who is love. He created us. He redeemed us. He left us His written instructions in the Bible. He will one day resurrect us to live in a perfect world.

No doubt about it: Jesus is the world's greatest lover.

Nail It Down: Read Revelation 21:3-4.

ONE LOVE

Gordon is 17, and Michelle (his sister) is 16. Both are Christians. If you could hide in their house and watch how they act, here's what you might see them doing on a typical day: arguing with their mom over their messy rooms; fighting over the TV and the use of the telephone; using each other's things without asking and rarely putting them back; each laughing when the other gets in trouble.

Both just endure the situation, assuming things will improve when they leave for college. If they'd enroll in Love U., things could improve today.

Course 102: The qualities of love

Look It Up: One of the most popular classes in the Master's program at Love U. is course 102, The Marks of Love, taught by Professor Paul. Here's the part of it that could help Gordon and Michelle:

"Love is patient, love is kind. It does not envy, it does not boast, it is not proud. It is not rude, it is not self-seeking, it is not easily angered, it keeps no record of wrongs. Love does not delight in evil but rejoices with the truth. It always protects, always trusts, always hopes, always perseveres. Love never fails" (1Corinthians 13:4-8).

Think It Through: Are all your relationships with other people marked by love? If you substituted your name for the word *love* in the passage just mentioned, would it be true?

How could Gordon and Michelle be more loving based on Professor Paul's description of love?

Work It Out: To determine the power of love in your life, rate yourself 1-10 (1= awful and 10= perfect) in these areas: patience __ ; kindness __ ; pride __ ; boastfulness __ ; rudeness __ ; selfishness __ ; anger __ ; tendency to hold grudges __ ; hatred of evil __ ; desire for truth __ ; perseverance __ trust __ ; willingness to protect __ ; hope for the best __ .

Now work on an area where you need improvement. For instance, if you're a 2 on the selfishness scale, take something you value (your time, money, or a possession) and donate it to a good cause like your local homeless shelter. Loan a blouse to your sister, or teach your kid brother how to skateboard.

Nail It Down: Read Romans 12:9-10.

Pray About It:

❤ ❤ ❤ ❤ ❤ T W O

Imagine the following situations:

1. You're in the middle of a major crisis. You ask your parents for support, and they respond: "Look, we're busy right now. 'The Cosby Show' is on. And afterwards we have to go to the store and pick up a few things. But, honey, we do love you. Really we do."

2. On the weekends your boyfriend or girlfriend is real affectionate and sweet, gushing about how much he or she loves you. But during the week he or she says, "Hey, what can I say? I just don't feel anything for you right now. Gimme some space, okay?"

Course 103: The demands of love

Look It Up: What a nightmare! And yet a lot of people actually think like that. Some imagine that love is shown merely by words. Others believe that love is just a feeling. When the feeling fades, the relationship is over. These people desperately need to take Love U. course 103, The Demands of Love.

In that class students find out that love is action. "Dear children, let us not love with words or tongue but with actions and in truth" (1 John 3:18).

Students there also discover that love is primarily a commitment, not a feeling—an action, not a goose-bump. God's love for the people of Israel was shown by His constant faithfulness to them, even when He was angered by their actions. (See Judges 10:6-16.)

Think It Through: What if God sat up in heaven and just kept saying over and over to the human race, "I love you," but He never did anything to show His love? What if His goodness to us depended on His feelings? What if He loved us only as long as we performed perfectly for Him?

The point? We need to be committed to doing loving actions for others even when we don't feel like it.

Work It Out: In each one of your close relationships (parents, siblings, special friends) show your love today by doing something. It doesn't have to cost money or take a lot of time. Try one of these: a note, a hug, a helping hand, a surprise, a sacrificial act, a thoughtful remembrance.

Remember: With love, talk is cheap and feelings are the result, not the goal. You do your part—performing acts of love—and the feelings will probably follow.

Nail It Down: Read John 13:34.

♥ ♥ ♥ ♥ ♥ ♥ THREE **LOVE** ♥ ♥ ♥ ♥ ♥ ♥ ♥ ♥

Stephanie Rockwell and Graham Lloyd, juniors at exclusive Hamilton Academy, claim to be in love. Maybe "in lust" is a better way to put it. See, their whole relationship revolves around heavy physical interaction. Take that away, and nothing's left.

• Justine, 14, met Rick, 17, at a youth meeting Friday night. Rick ended up taking her home.

Sunday morning, Justine announced that, yes, she is "in love with this gorgeous guy named Rick ... uh, well, I'm not sure what his last name is."

Course 104: Phony love

Look It Up: If these young people would sit through the Phony Love course at Love U., they might realize that what they're feeling is anything but love. Professor Paul demonstrates the bogus nature of lust:

"Put to death, therefore, whatever belongs to your earthly nature: sexual immorality, impurity, lust, evil desires. . . . As God's chosen people . . . put on love" (Colossians 3: 5-14).

Do you see the implication? The most sexually active person in the world can still miss out on love. Why? Because lust and love aren't the same thing. Lust is selfish. Love is self-less. Lust tears others down. But love respects and builds others up. (See 1 Corinthians 13.)

Think It Through: Is it possible to meet someone and immediately fall in love? No!

Genuine love is more than an exciting feeling. It is a commitment that grows and deepens even when the romantic fireworks and feelings fade away.

Work It Out: True love between a man and woman includes physical aspects that God created and blessed—no doubt about it! But phony love wants those aspects without the life-long commitment.

Here's the assignment for course 104:
• If you're involved in a no-holds-barred phony love relationship, stop! Ask your youth pastor, parents, best friend, anyone who will discourage you from continuing the relationship, to hold you accountable.
• If you aren't involved in phony love, ask God to give you the strength to obey Him in this area. By yourself, you're not above temptation; through Christ, you can resist!

Nail It Down: Read Job 31:1.

Pray About It: ───────────────────────

FOUR

Julie Holmes recently signed up for course 777, The Laboratory of Love.

Boy, was she surprised! She's no longer studying theories of love. Now Julie has to actually love several very unlovable people! Whether or not she gets her "Master's" degree depends on how well she does.

The professor, Dr. H. Spirit, assigned her to love three people: her stepfather ("I can't stand him!"), her lab partner ("What a geek!"), and the little kid next door ("He's possessed!"). Professor Spirit assured her He would help her, but Julie's not too thrilled.

Course 777: The laboratory of love

Look It Up: Jesus pointed out that it's no big deal to love the people who treat us right. Everybody does that. The hard part is loving those who aren't so nice.

"You have heard that it was said, 'Love your neighbor and hate your enemy.' But I tell you: Love your enemies and pray for those who persecute you" (Matthew 5:43-44).

Think It Through: Jesus commands us to love our enemies. We've talked a lot about acting in love. But how can we know if what we're doing is truly loving?

The Apostle John had a clear answer: "And this is love: that we walk in obedience to his commands" (2 John 6).

Work It Out: John says that love is defined by God's commands. Given John's definition of love, how can you love people you don't really feel good about?

If they're your parents (or others in authority over you), honor them with obedience and respect.

If they're your peers,
- show respect for their lives by, for example, driving safely and refusing to pick fights;
- show respect for their purity by refusing to tempt them to sexual sin;
- deal with them honestly and fairly, refusing to steal;
- tell them the truth;
- rejoice in their good fortune without envy or greed.

Those ideas aren't new; they're ancient. You'll find every one of them in the Ten Commandments, which are, according to John, the definition of love.

Nail It Down: Read Exodus 20. On Saturday, find out how some of these laws of love were applied in Israel by reading Exodus 22:1-14. On Sunday, read Psalm 19.

FIVE LOVE

HEAVEN

Have you ever wished that the world was a better place? A place where people were nicer to each other. A place where bad things didn't happen. A place where there were no hurts, pains, or disappointments. Sure you have. Everybody has.

A hunger for heaven. Everyone wishes for that kind of place, because we were created by God with a hunger for heaven in our hearts. Ecclesiastes 3:11 tells us that God has "set eternity in the hearts of men." We long for a perfect place, because we were made to live in just such a place. We were created for eternity, but because of sin we live in a world of suffering.

The presence of God. So what's heaven all about? It's been said that heaven will be like going to church for eternity. (That could be a scary thought, depending on what your church is like!) But the Bible says that heaven is the dwelling place of God (Matthew 6:9). Yet, heaven does not contain God—he cannot be confined to one place (1 Kings 8:27). Perhaps more than being a place, heaven is better described as the presence of God.

One day believers will live with God and there will be no more death, no more sorrow, no more sin, no more darkness (Revelation 21:3-4; 22:3-5). While we may have mental images about what heaven will be like— streets of gold, angelic choirs—the most important thing about heaven is that we will spend eternity in God's presence.

Heavenly citizens. We Christians need to remember that our true citizenship is in heaven (Philippians 3:20-21). This world is just our temporary residence. Our real home is the place for which we long—heaven.

No wonder Jesus says to store up treasures in heaven and not on earth! Our lives here and now are affected by our focus in life (Matthew 6:19-21).

Absolute fulfillment. Will your pet make it to heaven? Will you get to eat ice cream there?

All we can say is that heaven will be the fulfillment of the deepest longings of your heart. Once and for all, you will experience ultimate satisfaction in the presence of the One you were created to enjoy forever —your Father in heaven—God.

IF THE BIBLE REALLY IS TRUE...

If the Bible really is true, then . . .
God exists. Belief in a Creator isn't just wishful thinking or the leftover, mythical baggage of our superstitious ancestors. He's for real—holy, eternal, all-powerful, all-knowing, and personal. What's more, He loves you and wants you to know Him!

If the Bible really is true, then . . .
Sin is the human race's biggest problem. Sin isn't just a quaint, old-fashioned notion. It is a condition into which everyone is born, and it involves both rebellious attitudes and selfish actions. Sin is what keeps us from knowing God and finding real satisfaction in life. Permeating our lives, sin brings alienation and anguish—and if never dealt with, it leads to an eternity apart from God!

If the Bible really is true, then . . .
Jesus is the answer to our biggest problem. The ultimate solution to our needs isn't found in psychology, sociology, a strong economy, political maneuvering, or a clean environment. As sinners separated from God, we need forgiveness first and foremost. Only that will bring us back into a right relationship with God.

Through His death on the cross, Christ has provided that forgiveness. It is available. For you. Right now.

If the Bible really is true, then . . .
Real life begins with faith in Christ. It isn't enough to know about God or to occasionally think about His existence. Forgiveness and eternal life are granted when an individual looks at what Christ has done and sincerely says:

"Thank You, Lord, for dying for me. I admit I'm a sinner. Right now, I accept Your free gift of salvation. I'm trusting You to fill me with Your life and love. Make my life what You want it to be. Amen."

If the Bible really is true, then . . .
You can be a brand new person inside (2 Corinthians 5:17). What are you waiting for?

SPIRITUAL WARFARE ►►►►►

Boot Camp for Believers

"*Endure hardship with us like a good soldier of Christ Jesus*" (2 Timothy 2:3).

S pir•it•u•al (spir'i-choo-wal, chool), adj. 1. of the spirit or soul; not material 2. of or possessing the nature of spirit; incorporeal

war•fare (wor'fer), n. 1. hostilities; war; armed conflict 2. any kind of conflict

Spiritual warfare. You can't see it or hear it. But that doesn't mean it's not real. And that doesn't mean it won't affect you.

Are you ready for the battle with the Enemy?

If you aren't, you need to be; the Enemy is ready for you.

►►

Donny, Rhonda, and Katie are looking at a newsletter their youth pastor gave them. It's full of alarming news.

Item: Large numbers of Christian marriages are ending in divorce.

Item: Television preachers and local ministers are being caught in immorality.

Item: 60% of Christian teenagers report being sexually active.

Item: The incidences of occult worship and even murder are rising nationwide. In fact, pagan goddess worship is making a big comeback.

There's a war going on

Look It Up: From Genesis to Revelation, the Bible is clear: It's war out there! This ancient spiritual struggle is just as real as the physical conflicts that take place between nations. The Apostle Paul wrote:

"Finally, be strong in the Lord and in his mighty power. Put on the full armor of God so that you can take your stand against the devil's schemes. For our struggle is not against flesh and blood, but against the rulers, against the authorities, against the powers of this dark world and against the spiritual forces of evil in the heavenly realms" (Ephesians 6:10-12).

Think It Through: Most people and many Christians go through life unaware of the great conflict that's raging all around them. While they worry over trivial matters ("Did you see 'Cheers' last night?" or "Do you like this outfit better or this one?"), there's a worldwide war going on—with life-and-death consequences!

What would be the chance of survival for a deaf and blind person who stumbled across a raging battlefield, not even realizing a war was in progress?

Work It Out: This week is sort of like a boot camp for believers. The purpose is to make you more aware of the battle lines, and to show you how you can not only survive, but also succeed. Here's a prayer for the week:

"Lord, sometimes I get so caught up in activities that I forget there's an invisible war going on all around me. Help me this week to see that the conflict is real. Both sides are playing for keeps! Show me how to stand and fight the good fight of faith. I want to be victorious for Christ, who won the victory at the cross. Amen."

Nail It Down: Catch a glimpse of God's invisible armies—2 Kings 6:8-17.

➤➤➤➤➤➤➤➤➤ **ONE SPIRITUAL WARFAR**

The next day at school Donny and Katie overhear this conversation:

"Man, you missed the wildest movie!"

"Oh yeah? What's that?"

Revenge of the Devil's Daughter. It was unbelievable. This female demon slaughtered about 100 kids. There was blood everywhere! And they showed the devil too! He was totally evil. I'll be having nightmares for weeks . . . you gotta see it!"

"I'll check it out this weekend."

"I'll go with you."

How well do you know the Enemy?

Look It Up: Satan is not a product of some Hollywood special effects wizard. He's a dangerous killer.

• He is an angel who was expelled from heaven because of his rebellion against God's authority (Isaiah 14:12-14).

• He wants to destroy you. "Your enemy the devil prowls around like a roaring lion looking for someone to devour" (1 Peter 5:8).

• He met more than his match in the person of Jesus Christ: "Since the children have flesh and blood, he too shared in their humanity so that by his death he might destroy him who holds the power of death—that is, the devil—and free those who all their lives were held in slavery by their fear of death" (Hebrews 2:14-15).

Think It Through: We don't want to become obsessed with Satan, or be frightened by the verses that discuss his power. We learn about him only so we can be better equipped to stand against him until Christ returns.

Work It Out: If you've been dabbling in anything having to do with the occult—seances, tarot cards, crystals, astrology, a Ouija board, palm reading—stop immediately! Such practices are strictly forbidden in the Bible. (See Deuteronomy 18:10-13.)

But the devil doesn't restrict himself to the obvious occult. Some of his favorite arenas for distributing his deadly ideas are politics, education, and the media.

Pay careful attention to what you hear in school and from the news and entertainment media. Reject all beliefs and practices that give the devil a foothold in your life.

Nail It Down: Read 1 John 4:4.

Pray About It: ————

T W O

"That was awesome," Rhonda tells Katie.

"Yeah. Except now I really feel guilty."

The girls are riding home after youth group. The topic was spiritual warfare and the responsibility of each Christian to join the fight.

"The part that got me," Katie sighs, "was when Bill talked about being a soldier for Christ. He's right. Most of us are like Gomer Pyle—I know I am! We just bumble around and never get off of the military base and on the front lines."

Gomer Pyle or Rambo?

Look It Up: According to the Bible, Christians are soldiers in God's army—whether they like it or not. The question is, What kind of soldiers are we?

Are we concentrating on His cause? We need to be. "Endure hardship with us like a good soldier of Christ Jesus. No one serving as a soldier gets involved in civilian affairs—he wants to please his commanding officer" (2 Timothy 2:3-4).

Are we prepared for battle and keeping a sharp lookout for the enemy? That should be our mindset.

"Be self-controlled and alert" (1 Peter 5:8).

Think It Through: Good soldiers take advantage of their training. They obey orders and are concerned with only one thing: defeating the enemy.

Bad soldiers prefer the safety of the base. They follow orders only when they feel like it.

Which kind of soldier are you?

Work It Out: Take these steps to become a good soldier:
• Consider worship, youth group, and Bible study as training. Pay close attention. Take notes. Some of the information may one day save your life!
• Obey the orders of your Commander-in-Chief. These are found in His Word, the Bible.
• Make choices not on the basis of what is easiest, but on the basis of what is best. Good soldiers undertake any mission to insure victory.

Fourth, when an activity begins to divert your focus from the Lord and His work, reevaluate your priorities. Remember—military people can't afford to get caught up in nonmilitary business!

Nail It Down: Read Ephesians 6:18.

THREE **SPIRITUAL WARFAR**

H ere's what happened in the days after Katie told God she wanted to get turned around and start making a difference for Him at school.

When she told a friend in P.E. class about her decision, the friend responded, "Katie, quit being so righteous! Don't you think I saw you at that party last weekend?"

When she took an English exam, several kids were cheating. Katie felt an incredible temptation to join in. She did, and then the guilt really piled up.

Bracing for the Battle

Look It Up: Katie needs to know that God doesn't send his soldiers into battle unprotected.

"Put on the full armor of God, so that when the day of evil comes, you may be able to stand your ground, . . . Stand firm then, with the belt of truth buckled around your waist, with the breastplate of righteousness in place, and with your feet fitted with the readiness that comes from the gospel of peace. In addition to all this, take up the shield of faith, with which you can extinguish all the flaming arrows of the evil one. Take the helmet of salvation and the sword of the Spirit, which is the word of God" (Ephesians 6:13-17).

Think It Through: What good are weapons to a soldier if he leaves all this equipment in his tent when he goes out to fight? Are you using the divine weapons God has provided (2 Corinthians 10:3-5)?

Work It Out: Put on God's armor today and everyday.
• "The belt of truth"—Be a person of integrity and faithfulness. Honor your commitments.
• "The breastplate of righteousness"—Live a righteous life. It's a great protection (James 4:7).
• "Feet fitted with . . . the gospel of peace"—Be willing to take the gospel to the world.
• "The shield of faith"—Trust in the promises of God for security against the accusations and attacks of Satan.
• "The helmet of salvation"—The promise of salvation provides further confidence in battle.
• "The sword of the Spirit, which is the word of God"—This, the only offensive weapon, causes the enemy to flee (Matthew 4:1-11). Hang on to it and use it to God's glory!

Nail It Down: Read 1 Thessalonians 5:8.

Pray About It:

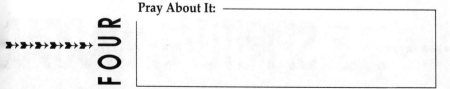

FOUR

>>>>>>>>>>

Despite a few setbacks (remember yesterday?), Katie stuck with her new commitment to Christ. She and Rhonda began meeting every morning to pray for each other. They agreed to read through the New Testament and to check up on each other every day.

Slowly but surely these two very normal girls are becoming battle-hardened soldiers for the Lord.

Through their witness they've each led a friend to the Savior! What's more, they're experiencing victory over the temptations that weeks before nailed them every time.

The outcome is never in doubt

Look It Up: Winning day-to-day battles is exciting. But even more exciting is the news that this fighting won't last forever! In our war against the forces of evil, God promises both protection and ultimate victory.

• "The Lord will rescue me from every evil attack and will bring me safely to his heavenly kingdom" (2 Timothy 4:18).

• "God is just: He will pay back trouble to those who trouble you and give relief to you who are troubled, and to us as well. This will happen when the Lord Jesus is revealed from heaven in blazing fire with his powerful angels (2 Thessalonians 1:6-7).

Think It Through: Even after the U.S. defeated Japan in World War II, many Japanese soldiers continued fighting on some of the islands in the Pacific. It took years to subdue some of these desperate men and finally end the conflict.

In the same way, Christ won the war against Satan at the Cross. The forces of evil were dealt the death blow when the Savior cried, "It is finished!" Now we're involved in the mop-up operation.

Work It Out: Spend some time thanking God that He has defeated the Enemy through the blood of His Son.

Meanwhile, find a friend and do what Rhonda and Katie are doing. Begin claiming the results of Christ's victory. Pray daily for each other and for friends who don't yet know the Lord. Think of creative ways to fight Christ's battles in your area of interest.

P.S. Don't forget to put on your armor!

Nail It Down: Read Romans 16:20. On Saturday, read Isaiah 53:11-12. On Sunday, read Isaiah 54:1-3 and Galatians 4:26-27 for the victorious results of the Cross.

FIVE SPIRITUAL WARFAR

40

DATING
Winning at the Dating Game

"Delight yourself in the LORD and he will give you the desires of your heart" (Psalm 37:4).

In some ways dating is like a game. You have to know certain rules. You get better by practicing a few fundamentals. You face intense competition. And finally, there are winners and losers. The problem is that when you "lose" at dating, it can hurt deeply and for a long time.

Join Kevin & Sheila and Pat & Amy this week as they go to dating "training camp." It's a week for every dater who feels rusty and needs a review of the basics.

After all, when it comes to dating, nobody wants to feel the "agony of defeat."

Amy is in shock. She is listening to Sheila turn down Ron Summers, the "Incredible Hunk" of Lincoln High, for a weekend date!

"Are you brain-dead?" Amy asks when Sheila hangs up the phone. "He looks exactly like Tom Cruise! Sheila, how could you?"

"I don't know. I just didn't feel right about it. I'm not sure he's a Christian."

"Sheila, life just isn't fair. I hardly ever get called. And here you are turning down Ron Summers! So what if he's not a Christian? He's not asking you to marry him!"

Have patience in the date wait

Look It Up: Amy's waiting for a call from anybody. Sheila's waiting for the right guy—a Christian guy. Who's right?

Consider these verses:

"Do not be yoked together with unbelievers. . . . What does a believer have in common with an unbeliever?" (2 Corinthians 6:14-15).

The phrase "yoked together" refers to the farming practice of hooking two animals side by side for the purpose of working together—perhaps pulling a plow. This passage tells us that Christians must not be paired with non-Christians in an intimate way.

Think It Through: In principle, a Christian's highest goal is to live according to the standards of truth and morality taught in the Bible (John 14:15). A non-Christian's highest goal is to live according to his or her own standards of truth and morality (Romans 3:10-18).

And so, for a Christian to seriously date a non-Christian is like yoking a mule and an ox together and then trying to plow a field. The two animals want to go in different directions and at different speeds.

Sheila is wise. She knows she could easily develop feelings for Ron. Then where would she be? In love with a guy who doesn't share her beliefs. In love with someone who might tempt her to drop her standards.

Work It Out: Resolve to date only committed Christians. You want to be intimately acquainted with only those who will build up your faith, not destroy it. Of course, you may (no, should) be friends with non-Christians. But beware of anything more serious than friendship!

Nail It Down: Read Ephesians 5:1-8.

ONE DATING

42

Sheila and Amy are talking about the same things most teenage girls talk about: love, sex, dating, and guys at school—not necessarily in that order. Let's listen in.

"Oh, Amy, at youth group last night we saw the best video on dating. Mainly it talked about what the Bible says . . . you know, the kind of people we should date and reasons for going out."

"Reasons? Do I need 'reasons'? I go out because that's what everyone does—to have fun, to keep from sitting home on weekends, to find a boyfriend. Aren't those reasons good enough?"

Know "why" before "who"

Look It Up: Amy asks a great question. What are good reasons for Christians to date? Try these:

1. To bring glory to God (1 Corinthians 10:31).
2. To encourage another Christian to grow: "And let us consider how we may spur one another on toward love and good deeds" (Hebrews 10:24).
3. To grow personally (Proverbs 27:17).
4. To prepare for marriage. As we date, we discover what kind of person would be best suited for us as a mate and how to relate well to the opposite sex.

Think It Through: Many students date for all the wrong reasons. Some date for sex and end up guilt ridden and under God's curse. Some date to find a steady and end up frustrated. Some date solely to have fun or to be seen with the right people or to keep from being bored—all reasons that won't bring satisfaction.

How would your dating life be changed if you adopted as your top priority to bring glory to God? If you were to take a sincere interest in others, being sensitive and encouraging to them while on dates, do you think you'd have a harder or easier time getting future dates?

Work It Out: Write out a list of reasons why you go (or would like to go) out on dates. Be honest. Which of these dating goals might bring disappointment?

Why not see dating from God's perspective? It's a great opportunity to bring glory to Him, to grow personally, to encourage others, and to lay a foundation for your future. Look at dating in that light and you'll have more genuine fun than you ever thought possible!

Nail It Down: Read Psalm 84:11.

Pray About It: ——————————————————

T W O

43

Pat and Kevin have it planned. They're going to double-date Saturday night—eat first and then go to a movie. All they need are dates!

Pat thumbs through the school yearbook. "Look, I'll call Carol if you'll call Karen."

"I don't know," Kevin replies.

"Kevin," Pat says, pointing to the yearbook, "we're talking two of the most awesome girls in the school."

"I know that. They're incredible looking! But that's not all that counts. Look, I'm tired of asking girls out just for the sake of going out. I want somebody really special."

In search of the perfect date

Look It Up: Maybe you can relate to Kevin's feelings. As you get older and grow as a Christian, you realize you want more in a date than someone with good looks, popularity, or lots of money.

What should a Christian look for in a potential date? Someone who takes seriously these words of Jesus: "Love the Lord your God with all your heart and with all your soul and with all your mind. . . . Love your neighbor as yourself" (Matthew 22:37-39).

In other words, the ideal person to date is someone
• who has a heart for God, someone who loves the Lord and is committed to walking with Him;
• who has a heart for people, someone who's unselfish and genuinely cares about others.

Think It Through: "But," you may argue, "if I only date serious Christians, I'll never have fun!" Wrong! Committed Christians can have more fun dating than anyone else!

Here's why: Knowing the rules and sticking to them frees both people to have an honest, genuine relationship with no emotional games. They can be themselves and enjoy each other.

Work It Out: Think back on the last three or four people you've dated. Are they really the kind of people God would have you date?

What about you? Are you living in a way that would be attractive to another committed Christian? What specific changes could you make that might make you more popular with the right kind of people?

Nail It Down: 2 Timothy 2:22
P. S. Kevin finally called Sheila for the big weekend. And Pat got a date with Sheila's friend Amy.

THREE **DATING**

Kevin and Pat are stumped. They've got dates with Sheila and Amy for Saturday night, but their plan to go eat and see a movie is ruined.

Both girls have already seen the only decent movie playing in town! And they have to be at the school auditorium by 5:00 P.M. for a Latin Club banquet!

"Amy said we can pick them up at 7:00," Pat sighs, "but they won't be hungry and they've already seen the movie. What are we going to do?"

Dinner and a show—no, no, no!

Look It Up: Christians don't have to keep doing the same old things over and over again on dates. Why? For this reason: "God created man in his own image" (Genesis 1:27).

Because we are made in God's image, we have the God-given ability to be creative. We can come up with different ideas. We can try new things. We can be unique. And believe it or not, this is true for everyone.

Think It Through: Let's play "create-a-date." Think of unique things you could do on a date that would please God, enable you to get to know your date, and provide hours of fun.

Here's just a partial list: jog, play tennis, play ping-pong, swim, play basketball, cook, visit a nursing home, wash your car, ride bikes, visit people in the hospital, go to a historical site, visit a museum, take a walk, look at stars, take pictures, make your own video movie, watch people at the airport, pray together, do a Bible study, have a barbeque, paint, write poetry or songs or letters, ski, volunteer to do charitable work together, go witnessing, go to a public lecture, play board games, build something, feed ducks, learn a new skill, go to the zoo, go to the library, or read to each other.

Work It Out: On a scale of 1–10 (one being boring and 10 exciting), rate your last five dating activities. Are you using the creative ability God has given you?

Think of 10 creative dates you could do for under $10. Now, don't just sit there. Get to work on your creative date plans!

Nail It Down: Reflect on God's creativity in Psalm 145:11-12.

Pray About It: _____

FOUR

⛵ ⛵ ⛵ ⛵ ⛵

45

It's 11:00 P.M. on Saturday night and Kevin & Sheila and Pat & Amy are having a great time!

The guys got creative and went to Kevin's for a cake-baking contest. The girls died laughing as they watched the guys stumble all over the kitchen.

Now Pat and Kevin are in the bathroom getting flour out of their hair. Pat is so excited he's about to explode: "Man, Amy is the greatest! Did you see how she keeps smiling at me? Kevin, no kidding, this is love at first sight—well, at least at first 'date'! Maybe I'll give her my senior ring next week!"

Romance is a risky business!

Look It Up: Almost nothing can compare to the feeling of going out with someone and having everything click. But what about going steady so soon? What about going steady anytime? Here are some Biblical responses to those who go steady only

- for security—Only in God is there true security (Psalm 91:1-2);
- for increased sexual involvement—"Flee from sexual immorality"(1 Corinthians 6:18);
- because of infatuation—Sometimes our feelings can trick us into thinking we're in love when we're really not: "The heart is deceitful above all things and beyond cure" (Jeremiah 17:9).

Think It Through: Here are other things to consider:
- Are you old enough? (It takes real maturity to correctly handle a steady relationship.)
- Do your parents approve? (Their support makes all the difference.)
- Whom are you considering? (A solid Christian for a boyfriend or girlfriend can help you grow. But someone who's not excited about the Lord can hurt your walk.)
- Is God glorified by your relationship? (If it's not His will, it's certain to fail.)

Work It Out: Evaluate your relationship based on the Biblical principles we've noted. Are your motives for going steady really good ones?

Write out what you think a really good, Christ-centered dating relationship would be like. Resolve to have only that kind of relationship.

Nail It Down: Read 1 Thessalonians 4:1. On Saturday, read 1 Timothy 3:1-4, a description of a godly man. On Sunday, read 1 Peter 3:1-6 about a godly woman.

FIVE DATING

FIVE

✪✪✪✪✪✪ IDENTITY ✪✪✪✪✪✪✪✪✪
The Marks of a Christian

Meet Kent Clark, part-time, mild-mannered sophomore reporter for the Metropolis High School *Gazette* and full-time "Super-Christian."

Why is Kent able to have such a big influence for the Lord at his school? Is it because he's more talented, or smarter, or because he acts holier than everyone else? No!

Kent's just an ordinary guy who believes in an extraordinary God. He understands the marks that give a person a Christian identity—and he does his best to wear them.

The results?

Well, what else can we say? They're "super"!

"Live a life worthy of the calling you have received" (Ephesians 4:1).

✪✪✪✪✪✪✪✪✪✪✪✪✪✪✪✪✪✪✪✪✪✪✪✪✪

You are the salt of the earth

Kent Clark's first assignment was to write a feature story called "Alcohol & Metropolis High School."

Kent's research showed that 85% of the student body said they drank regularly, and 42% admitted to getting drunk at least once a week. Shocked, Kent prayed, "Lord, I want to be salt for you at this school."

Over the year, by praying regularly about the situation, by writing several editorials, and by sponsoring some nonalcoholic "alternative parties," Kent and his friends saw alcohol become less of a big deal on campus.

Look It Up: Kent had an impact on his school because he remembered these words of Jesus Christ:

"You are the salt of the earth. But if the salt loses its saltiness, how can it be made salty again? It is no longer good for anything, except to be thrown out and trampled by men" (Matthew 5:13).

Think It Through: We can understand Jesus' statement in two ways:
• Salt was used in New Testament times (and even now in countries lacking adequate refrigeration) as a preservative to cure meat and prevent it from spoiling.
• Salt creates thirst.

In other words, when we Christians live as we are supposed to live, we keep society from decaying. We also make nonbelievers "thirsty"—thirsty to know why we are different.

Are you a salty Christian or have you lost your flavor?

Work It Out: According to the words of Christ, you most certainly can influence your world today. Like Kent, you can take a stand against some evil in society and do something about it.

You can't do everything, so pick a problem—drug abuse, abortion, pornography, obscenity, world hunger, homelessness, illiteracy—and commit to work diligently until the battle is won.

At the same time, as you live for the Lord, others will be thirsty to know why you're different. Use these opportunities to be a witness for Him.

Nail It Down: Read Colossians 4:5-10.

ONE IDENTITY

Kent hadn't been working on the school paper very long when two amazing things happened.

First, during an editorial meeting the staff got into a big discussion about religion. Kent was surprised: No one else claimed to be a Christian, but several people seemed interested in spiritual matters.

Second, at a state-wide, newspaper workshop, Kent found out he'd be rooming with Carl Thomas, one of the guys most interested in God.

As they lugged their bags into the hotel, Kent thought, "Lord, I want to be a light for You this weekend."

You are the light of the world

Look It Up: Kent prayed that prayer because he remembered these words of Christ:

"You are the light of the world. A city on a hill cannot be hidden. Neither do people light a lamp and put it under a bowl. Instead they put it on its stand, and it gives light to everyone in the house. In the same way, let your light shine before men, that they may see your good deeds and praise your Father in heaven" (Matthew 5:14-16).

Think It Through: Think of pitching a tent at night without the aid of a lantern or walking down a dark trail without a flashlight. You'd be stumbling, fumbling, and completely lost without some sort of light to illumine your way! Light reveals, guides, and provides comfort.

In the same way, Christians are lights in a dark world. By shining for Christ and letting His life and love radiate through our lives, we point lost people to the proper path.

Work It Out: How do we shine for God in a dark world? By doing what Jesus called "good deeds." Everything we say and do should reflect our love for God and our care for others. Here are some specific and practical good deeds you can do today:

• Run an errand for someone who's sick.
• Take some toys and old clothes to the Salvation Army or Goodwill.
• Contribute your allowance to the local Crisis Pregnancy Center.
• Get your youth group to sponsor an after-school program for kids with working mothers.

Pick one of these projects and start shining!

Nail It Down: Read Daniel 12:3.

Pray About It:

✪ ✪ ✪ ✪ ✪ TWO

What's the deal with this Kent Clark guy? What's his secret?

While most Christians in Metropolis see nothing exciting happening in their spiritual lives, it seems that Kent is always in the middle of something.

Let's eavesdrop on his prayer time and see if we can find out his secret: ". . . and Your Word is so true. You are the Good Shepherd! O, Lord, help me realize that You'll keep me safe and provide everything I need if I'll just stay close to You. Thank You for loving me in Christ my Lord. Amen."

You are God's sheep

Look It Up: Kent had these verses in mind when he was talking to God:

• "The LORD is my shepherd, I shall not be in want. He . . . leads me beside quiet waters, he restores my soul. He guides me in paths of righteousness for his name's sake" (Psalm 23:1-3).

• "Come, let us bow down in worship, let us kneel before the LORD our Maker; for he is our God and we are the people of his pasture, the flock under his care" (Psalm 95:6-7).

What a great analogy! Like a shepherd, God lovingly cares for us, His flock. In Him, we "sheep" find nourishment, guidance, and rest.

Think It Through: According to Phillip Keller, a former shepherd, sheep are dependent animals. As long as they remain close to their owner, they enjoy prosperity, protection, and peace. However, as soon as they wander away from their keeper, they open themselves up to danger and possible death.

As a sheep, are you listening to and staying close to the Good Shepherd? If not, why not?

Work It Out: A big part of Kent's spiritual success is the fact that he begins each day expressing both his dependence on God and his desire to walk closely with God.

Go to your local Christian bookstore or to your church library and get one of Phillip Keller's books, either *A Shepherd Looks at Psalm 23* or *A Shepherd Looks at the Good Shepherd and His Sheep*. These books are easy to read and are filled with insights about what it means to be a sheep in God's flock.

(And why not pray the prayer that Kent prayed?)

Nail It Down: Read John 10:1-18.

✪ ✪ ✪ ✪ ✪ ✪ THREE **IDENTITY** ✪ ✪ ✪ ✪ ✪ ✪

For several weeks this spring, Kent and his girlfriend, Lois, began to get out of control in their physical relationship. Soon Kent noticed that he was often getting depressed. And then he started thinking, "If I really am a Christian, would I be acting like this?"

While on a spring retreat a couple of weeks later, Kent realized that God demands (not suggests) obedience. So, he got down on his knees and said, "Lord, I am truly sorry. Forgive me for my foolishness." That was the end of Kent and Lois's late night "couch wrestling."

You are God's container

Look It Up: What Kent realized is this truth: God will not bless someone involved in willful disobedience.

"In a large house there are articles not only of gold and silver, but also of wood and clay; some are for noble purposes and some for ignoble. If a man cleanses himself from the latter, he will be an instrument for noble purposes, made holy, useful to the Master and prepared to do any good work" (2 Timothy 2:20-21).

In this passage, Paul urged his young friend Timothy to guard against outer corruption (at the hands of false teachers) and to develop inner purity.

Think It Through: The Greek word translated "article" in the passage above is translated elsewhere in the New Testament as "jar" (Luke 8:16) and "pottery" (Revelation 2:27). In other words, Paul is talking about various household containers.

Would you want to drink out of a cup that had old coffee grounds and mold growing in it? Would you want to toss a green salad in the family garbage can?

If God isn't using you right now, could it be that there is some filth in your life that needs cleaning up?

Work It Out: Do you want to be useful to God? Do you want to be prepared for whatever situation He might bring your way? Then clean up your act on a daily basis. Here's how:

• Ask Him to show you any sin in your life that needs to be dealt with (Psalm 139:23).

• Admit your failures, turning away from them and back to God (1 John 1:9).

• Ask God to use you to accomplish His work (2 Timothy 2:21)

Nail It Down: Read 2 Corinthians 7:1.

Pray About It: _____

✪ ✪ ✪ ✪ ✪ FOUR

51

As his youth group planned their big Christmas program with music and drama, Kent felt more and more depressed.

"I can't sing! I can't act! I'm not artistic enough even to get the scenery ready! Nothing's left!"

"Why don't you try the refreshment committee?" Lois suggested.

"Yeah, right! You want the church to get sued for food poisoning?"

"Kent!" Mr. Dawson barked. "Quit focusing on what you can't do, and look at what you can contribute. Do a story for the school newspaper!"

You are part of the body of Christ

Look It Up: The Bible makes this same point: Every believer is a valuable part of the body of Christ:

"The body is a unit, . . . and though all its parts are many, they form one body. So it is with Christ. . . . God has arranged the parts in the body, every one of them, just as he wanted them to be. . . . The eye cannot say to the hand, 'I don't need you!' And the head cannot say to the feet, 'I don't need you!' On the contrary, those parts of the body that seem to be weaker are indispensable" (1 Corinthians 12:12, 18, 21-22).

Think It Through: Everyone can't be a star. Where would the quarterback be without his linemen, the equipment manager, the trainer? Where would an actress be without the costume designer, the lighting director, the special effects people, the make-up artists?

You're an important part of Christ's body! (If you don't think so, consider how much your whole body hurts and is affected when you stub your little toe.)

Work It Out: If you want to make a difference for Christ in your community, quit comparing yourself to everyone else and do what God has gifted you to do.

If you sing, do that as well as you know how. If setting up chairs before the meetings is what you do best, go for it! If you can best help by typing for your youth pastor, type your fingers off!

The point is to figure out where you fit, and get involved. That's how Christians will best affect our world—by working together like a disciplined team.

Nail It Down: Read Romans 12:4-8. On Saturday, read Acts 2:42-47 for an example of real "body life." On Sunday, read Psalm 133. (But please don't pour oil on your youth pastor's head!)

✦✦✦✦✦✦ FIVE IDENTITY ✦✦✦✦✦✦

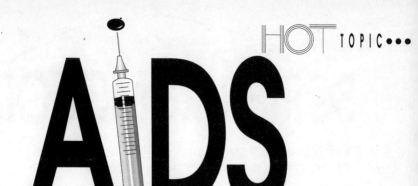

AIDS

Polls say it scares us more than almost anything else. And it should. We don't know where it came from, exactly who is infected, or all the ways it can be spread. We only know that it kills 100 percent of its victims. "It" is AIDS, the deadly epidemic that's sweeping the globe.

Prevention. Researchers agree that most AIDS cases arise after engaging in promiscuous sex (whether homosexual or heterosexual) or sharing a dirty needle when using drugs. A smaller percentage of victims have been infected by receiving contaminated blood, or by being the spouse or child of a sexually active person or drug user. Therefore, most doctors now agree that by abstaining from premarital sex and remaining faithful after marriage, one can radically reduce the chances of contracting the AIDS virus. Isn't it interesting that sexual purity is what God's Word has always commanded (1 Corinthians 6:9, 18; Colossians 3:5)?

Education. Even so, many persons don't like the idea of abstaining from sex. They want to be immoral—without the risk of AIDS. This explains the popularity of the term "safe sex." However, the argument for "safe sex" ignores a critical point: The only sex that can truly be safe is sex according to God's standard—one sexual partner (of the opposite sex) for life in Christian marriage. The objective in AIDS education, therefore, should not be to tell people how to make illicit sex 100 percent safe—an impossible goal anyway—but patiently explaining why only sex as God intended it can truly be safe.

Compassion. AIDS victims are usually treated like the vilest of sinners, like modern-day lepers. Sadly, God's people are often the quickest to judge and condemn. As those who know the love and compassion of Christ, we must respond to these desperate and dying individuals in a way that pleases God. We must pray that researchers find a cure. We must pray for a way to reach out to those who have nowhere else to turn. If Christians are callous towards those with AIDS, we are no better than the self-righteous Pharisees of Jesus' day who looked with contempt on their society's sick and wretched. See John 8:1-11; Mark 1:40-42; and Mark 2:13-17 for examples of how Jesus treated the helpless and hopeless.

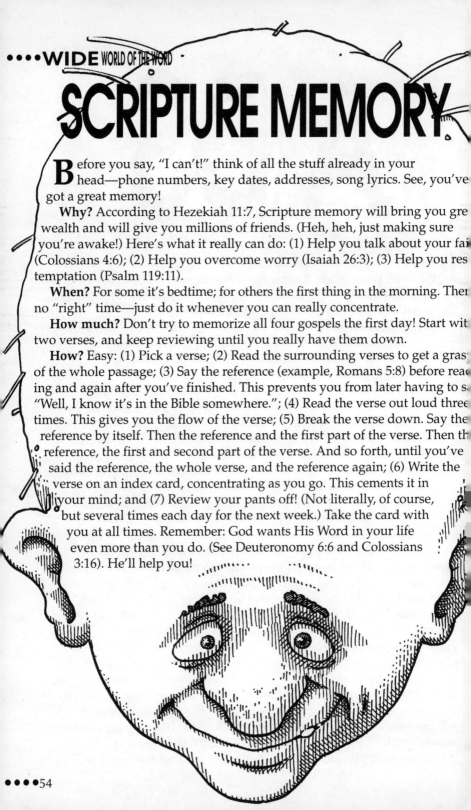

SCRIPTURE MEMORY

Before you say, "I can't!" think of all the stuff already in your head—phone numbers, key dates, addresses, song lyrics. See, you've got a great memory!

Why? According to Hezekiah 11:7, Scripture memory will bring you gre wealth and will give you millions of friends. (Heh, heh, just making sure you're awake!) Here's what it really can do: (1) Help you talk about your fai (Colossians 4:6); (2) Help you overcome worry (Isaiah 26:3); (3) Help you res temptation (Psalm 119:11).

When? For some it's bedtime; for others the first thing in the morning. Ther no "right" time—just do it whenever you can really concentrate.

How much? Don't try to memorize all four gospels the first day! Start wit two verses, and keep reviewing until you really have them down.

How? Easy: (1) Pick a verse; (2) Read the surrounding verses to get a gras of the whole passage; (3) Say the reference (example, Romans 5:8) before read ing and again after you've finished. This prevents you from later having to s "Well, I know it's in the Bible somewhere."; (4) Read the verse out loud three times. This gives you the flow of the verse; (5) Break the verse down. Say the reference by itself. Then the reference and the first part of the verse. Then th reference, the first and second part of the verse. And so forth, until you've said the reference, the whole verse, and the reference again; (6) Write the verse on an index card, concentrating as you go. This cements it in your mind; and (7) Review your pants off! (Not literally, of course, but several times each day for the next week.) Take the card with you at all times. Remember: God wants His Word in your life even more than you do. (See Deuteronomy 6:6 and Colossians 3:16). He'll help you!

FEAR
Freedom from F-f-fear

You're in a maze with dozens of passageways. You're not sure where any of them leads. So you take a quick left, then a right. Suddenly you're face to face with your biggest fear.

What is it? The future? Rejection? Failure? Death? Disaster? Disease? Something irrational? God? What are the things that frighten you most?

This week we're going to learn how to face those fears head-on. Because life can seem like a maze. And you never know what you might meet around the next corner.

"Do not fear, for I am with you; do not be dismayed, for I am your God. I will strengthen you and help you; I will uphold you with my righteous right hand" (Isaiah 41:10).

A nna! Oh,
  Anna! Anna,
are you listening to
me? Anna, turn off
that TV and listen
to me."

"No, I don't
want to."

"Why not?"

"Because I don't
like you. You're
scary."

"But, Anna,
don't you know
who I am? Why,
I'm your own
future, for goodness
sakes! Can't we just
talk? We've got to
discuss what your
plans are. Where
are you going?
What do you want
to do?"

"I don't know.
Go away!"

Frightened by the future

Look It Up: Maybe you're like Anna—scared of what lies ahead. If so, you're not alone. Look at Psalm 34. Even David felt fearful and uncertain about the future.

Here's the background of the psalm: David had been anointed as the future king. As a result, jealous King Saul, the reigning monarch, was trying to kill him. Abandoned and terrified, David sat in a cave wondering what the future held (see 1 Samuel 22:1 and 23:10).

Not until David turned to God—"I sought the LORD, and he answered me; he delivered me from all my fears" (Psalm 34:4)—and remembered God's goodness—"Taste and see that the LORD is good; blessed is the man who takes refuge in him" (Psalm 34:8)—was David able to come to grips with his fear.

Think It Through: Take a look at the good side of fear: While jogging, you are chased by a vicious dog. Suddenly, you are a world-class sprinter. Covering 100 yards in 10 seconds, you jump a six foot fence!

Then there's the bad side of fear: Like Anna, you let fear (in this case, fear of the future) paralyze you. You focus on the situation rather than on the solution.

Work It Out: Are you afraid of your future? Freaked out by the thought of college or career? Scared you won't find happiness? Why not follow David's lead?

1. Seek the Lord. Tell Him about your worries and ask Him to deliver you from these fears.

2. Remember God's goodness. He's not interested in playing cosmic games with your emotions. The good God who called His creation "good" cares deeply about His people. (Claim the promise of Romans 8:32. It's an amazing verse!)

Nail It Down: Read Matthew 6:25-34.

********** ONE FEAR ****************

56

John unzips his gym bag and removes his sweaty practice uniform. He stares intensely at the words on the shirt, "Collins High Basketball." All of a sudden he's not alone.

"You're not gonna make first team, you know," says Failure. "You don't have a chance. Your Dad's really gonna hang his head in shame. Wasn't he all-district?"

"Yeah," says John.

"Face it, dude. Not only will your dad be ver-r-r-y dis-appointed, but no girl—especially Shannon—wants to go out with a guy who sits on the bench."

Failure & rejection are gruesome

Look It Up: In Psalm 27 David describes a time when he was surrounded by enemies. He had every reason to feel fearful. He might have been tempted to think, "I'm a failure. See how the people hate me? They've totally rejected me!" But he didn't. Notice his amazing confidence:

"The LORD is my light and my salvation. . . . The LORD is the stronghold of my life. . . . Though an army besiege me, my heart will not fear; though war break out against me, even then I will be confident" (Psalm 27:1, 3).

The implication? "God hasn't rejected me. Therefore, I don't have to be afraid!"

Think It Through: A junior named Bob has amazing confidence. He calls any girl he wants to date, has run for student government, has tried out for several parts in school plays, and has gone out for three athletic teams. He's failed a lot and succeeded a few times. Why is he so fearless?

Because God is the most important Person in Bob's life. Bob knows God loves him and will protect him. That knowledge gives Bob the freedom to be bold.

Work It Out: Don't let failure bully you around! Let God be your bodyguard and best friend. He loves and accepts you—even if you fail.

This week do something you always wanted to do but have never attempted because of the fear of failure or rejection. Go out for a team, run for an office, call a person you'd like to get to know, interview for a better job. Even if you don't make it, hey, at least you gave it a shot! You haven't lost a thing. And if you do make it, you'll have a great chance to shine for the Lord!

Nail It Down: Read Romans 8:38-39.

Pray About It:

******** TWO

Last night the news anchor reported one scary story after another. He talked about the continuing spread of AIDS. He mentioned the fear that some Middle Eastern radicals might have nuclear weapons.

Then he talked about the hole in the ozone layer, the increasing pollution in the oceans, and the new fears of another stock-market collapse. Another report predicted a major earthquake in California.

Today, Candy feels afraid. She thinks, "I don't want to die. I haven't done everything I want to do."

On your knees before the three D'

Look It Up: Death. Disaster. Disease. Does the Bible give Christians any sort of comfort against these devastating destroyers that strike savagely and suddenly?

You bet.

• "Even though I walk through the valley of the shadow of death, I will fear no evil, for you are with me; your rod and your staff, they comfort me" (Psalm 23:4).

• "God is our refuge and strength, an ever-present help in trouble. Therefore we will not fear, though the earth give way and the mountains fall into the heart of the sea" (Psalm 46:1-2).

• "If calamity comes upon us, whether the sword of judgment, or plague or famine, we . . . will cry out to you in our distress, and you will hear us and save us" (2 Chronicles 20:9).

Think It Through: Do these verses mean that Christians are exempt from death, disaster, and disease? No. But they do assure us that no matter what we face, God is holding our hand and leading us through to victory.

Work It Out: You have two choices today. You can play the "What if?" game—What if I somehow get AIDS? What if there is a nuclear war? What if my parents get killed?—and scare yourself silly. Or you can walk with God and trust that He is good enough and powerful enough to do the right thing.

Here's a prayer for everyone who fears any of the three D's: "Lord, sometimes the world is a scary place. You understand that. Help me to not be so fearful. Teach me to focus on You, the Problem-solver, who will one day put an end to all problems, rather than on death, disaster, and disease. Amen."

Nail It Down: Read Hebrews 2:14-15.

********* THREE **FEAR** ***************

More common than people named Smith, the scary members of Phobia family pop up everywhere. Perhaps you recognize some of them. Maybe one of them has even been attacking you.

There's demophobia (fear of crowds); musophobia (fear of mice); belonephobia (fear of needles); astraphobia (fear of lightning); gephyrophobia (fear of crossing a bridge); and about a couple hundred others. There's even one named arachibutyrophobia (the fear of peanut butter sticking to the roof of your mouth)!

Look out for the phobia family

Look It Up: Are you familiar with any of those characters? More than you'd care to be? Look at Psalm 55.

While not a detailed psychology text about dealing with specific fears, this passage does describe a terribly frightened man—David.

"My heart is in anguish within me. . . . Fear and trembling have beset me; horror has overwhelmed me. I said, 'Oh, that I had the wings of a dove! I would fly away and be at rest' " (Psalm 55:4-6).

The psalm also shows that David ultimately finds peace. How? By realizing that God hears his cries (vv. 16-17) and by remembering that God is faithful (vv. 22-23).

Think It Through: These kinds of fears may seem silly to you, but they're no joke to the 2 to 4 percent of the population who suffer from them.

How would you help someone struggling with one of these fears?

Work It Out: Phobias are irrational fears that cause intense hatred of the object of the fear.

Here are some phobias you won't find listed in any psychology textbook:
• Theophobia—the irrational fear and hatred of God
• Christophobia—the irrational fear and hatred of Jesus Christ
• Nomophobia—the irrational fear and hatred of God's law (Nomos is the Greek word for law.)

Here's the bad news: Everyone starts out with these phobias (Romans 1:18-32). Here's the good news: Christ can wash them away.

Have you asked Christ to wash your phobias away?

Nail It Down: Read Psalm 56:3.

Pray About It:

******** **FOUR**

Mollie's greatest fear? God. How come, Mollie?

"I don't know. Sometimes I just get the feeling that He's gonna zap me. I mean, if you read through the Bible, it seems like He's always ticked off at somebody."

Lance, on the other hand, thinks of God as "the Man upstairs." If you ask him, Lance will tell you how glad he is to have a buddy like "the Big G."

Which attitude is right—being scared to death of God, or treating him like a cool dude?

Fearing your heavenly Father

Look It Up: Neither! Yes, the Bible does say we should fear God. But the fear that believers are to have for God is more like the obedient awe and respect one has for a powerful head of state like a president or a queen, rather than the terror a prisoner of war has for his captor.

"The LORD Almighty is the one you are to regard as holy, he is the one you are to fear, he is the one you are to dread" (Isaiah 8:13).

Such a reverential attitude keeps us from sin (Exodus 20:20), brings blessing in our lives (Proverbs 22:4), and draws us closer to God (Psalm 103:11, 17).

This healthy fear is the result of remembering that one day we will appear before the judgment seat of Christ (2 Corinthians 5:10; Revelation 14:7).

Think It Through: If you were to attend a banquet at the White House, would you slap the President on the back? Would you tell a crude joke to Billy Graham? How much more honor does our awesome God deserve?

Work It Out: The command to "fear the Lord" means that we approach God humbly, with deep respect and honor.

To develop a healthy fear of God, you need to be a faithful reader of the Bible (Deuteronomy 31:12-13).

To show this fear of God, you need to be a faithful doer of the Bible (Deuteronomy 6:2).

For extra help in learning to fear the Lord, copy Psalm 147:11 on an index card and carry it around with you all day today. It's a great verse!

Nail It Down: Read 1 John 4:18. (This verse talks about the wrong kind of fear.) On Saturday, read Psalm 130:3-4. Notice: The right kind of fear follows forgiveness. On Sunday, read Psalm 130:3-4 again—and memorize it.

********** FIVE **FEAR** ****************

AUTHORITY
The War of Independence

"Humble yourselves before the Lord, and he will lift you up" (James 4:10).

Pick the statement that doesn't belong:
1. "Get off my back!"
2. "Freedom means doing whatever I want."
3. "Nobody tells me what to do!"
4. "I'll respect and submit to your authority."

In a defiant world, you don't hear that last statement too often. In fact, it's natural to resent and reject the authorities over us, rather than submit to them.

In your own war for independence, declare a truce. Discover that there are alternatives to rebellion. It could be one of the best decisions you'll ever make.

Chuck's family has always been actively involved in church. But about a year ago his mom died in a car wreck.

Now Chuck is extremely bitter.

He says, "My mom really loved God, and look what she got in return. God calls Himself loving, but He doesn't even pro-tect the people who follow Him. What a joke! I'm telling you, it doesn't pay to try to live for Him. From now on, I'm doing whatever I feel like doing."

Don't fight Him; He's on your side!

Look It Up: It's understandable that Chuck would be grieving after his loss. But grieving is one thing; judging God is another. Chuck is really saying, "If God does things my way, I'll cooperate. I'll even love Him. But as soon as He allows something tragic to happen in my life, I'll no longer do what He says. In fact, I'll hate Him."

Chuck's plan will never work.

" 'God opposes the proud but gives grace to the humble.' Submit yourselves, then, to God. Resist the devil, and he will flee from you. Come near to God and he will come near to you" (James 4:6-8).

Think It Through: If God is the absolute authority in the universe, do you think He's willing to settle for having limited authority in the lives of His children?

People rebel against God's authority for all sorts of reasons, not just when they experience tragedy. Some people who have been blessed with all kinds of good things still reject God's authority in their lives.

Either way, they miss this important truth: God is not a cosmic tyrant who arbitrarily orders people around just for the sake of exercising authority. He's a loving heavenly Father who gives us commands and rules for our own benefit. By submitting, we win, not lose!

Work It Out: Have you been rebelling against God in some area of your life? Why not quit fighting a losing, pointless battle?

• Admit your pride, asking God to root it out of your life (James 4:6).

• Submit to God, recognizing His lordship in your life (James 4:7).

• Cultivate a closer walk with Him to guard against future rebelliousness (James 4:8).

Nail It Down: Read Proverbs 29:23.

ONE AUTHORITY

As her date drives away, Chrissy checks her watch—1:15 A.M. She gulps, remembering her dad's words earlier: "Be home by midnight."

"Maybe they're asleep," she thinks. Then her heart sinks. Her dad is at the door.

"Young lady, do you know how much your mother and I have been worrying about you?"

"Good grief, Dad. I'm 17 years old. What's the big deal?"

"Watch your mouth, Chris. As long as you're under our roof, you'll play by our rules. You can forget your plans for the next two weeks."

The other side of parent problems

Look It Up: Almost nothing eats at us more than the idea that our parents can boss us around. But look at it from their perspective. God "bosses them around" with regard to how they raise us. He says:

"Train a child in the way he should go, and when he is old he will not turn from it" (Proverbs 22:6).

God expects parents to discipline (Proverbs 23:13), to teach (Deuteronomy 6:6-7), to provide (1 Timothy 5:8).

Whew! No wonder parents are sometimes so uptight!

Think It Through: God has instituted several "community units" in His world, each with leaders who are to represent God. Some of these God-ordained community units are the government (Romans 13:1-5), the church (Matthew 16:19), the workplace (Ephesians 6:5-9), and (you guessed it) the family (Ephesians 6:1-4).

In all of these community units, people under authority are to submit to their leaders unless their leaders command them to do something forbidden by God, or forbid them to do something commanded by God.

Since God has given your parents authority in your family and also commanded you to submit to their authority, whom are you ultimately rebelling against when you rebel against your parents?

Work It Out: Freak your mom and dad out this week by submitting to their authority with no arguments, no discussions. Don't explain your little experiment; just do it until they ask, "Are you feeling okay?"

Besides the fun of seeing their reaction, your obedience will make for better relations on the homefront—and hopefully become your permanent response.

Nail It Down: Read Colossians 3:20.

Pray About It:

TWO

63

Mrs. Barden is a twelfth-grade history teacher who's as tough as nails. In spite of her size (about 5'1") and her age (about 200), she exercises total control in the classroom.

While lecturing on the causes of the Civil War, she is interrupted twice by Keith and Ronnie who are whispering in the corner.

"Okay, guys, that's it. I warned you once. I'll see you both after school in detention hall."

"C'mon, Mrs. Barden, we've got basketball practice."

"Hmmm. I guess you'll be late, won't you?"

Showing class in the classroom

Look It Up: Have you ever had a teacher like that? You're tempted to think, "She can't do that!" What is the proper response to authority figures at school?

• Submit in order to learn. "Instruct a wise man and he will be wiser still; teach a righteous man and he will add to his learning" (Proverbs 9:9).

• Submit in order to be a witness to non-Christian teachers (Colossians 4:5).

• Submit in order to show respect (1 Peter 2:17).

• Submit in order to be an example to other Christians (Titus 2:7).

As you can see, by submitting you please God, make friends for Christ, and influence others. How can something that does all that be a bad deal?

Think It Through: Sometimes teachers get a little power crazy. Others are unfair on occasion. But humble submission to their authority will always produce better results than a cocky, defiant, rebellious attitude.

Your parents have delegated responsibility to your school. If your teachers represent your parents, and your parents represent God, who are you ultimately rebelling against if you rebel against your teachers?

Work It Out: If you get along with your teachers, great! Keep working at having good relationships with them by respecting their authority.

If you've had a clash with a teacher, write him or her a short note something like this: "I realize that I acted pretty cocky in your class. Please forgive me for challenging your authority."

Sure, that will be tough. Sometimes it's tough to do what's right.

Nail It Down: Read Proverbs 13:10.

THREE AUTHORITY

Brent and a carload of guys were making their way (a bit recklessly) to meet up with everyone else after the game. Suddenly, in the rear-view mirror Trent spotted some flashing blue lights.

Within a minute, a couple of older policemen were checking IDs and shining flashlights in scared faces.

After a few moments of silence, Bobby, one of the older guys in the group, smirked to the nearest officer, "C'mon, man, it's not like we're out robbing banks. Why don't you guys relax?"

You can imagine how well that went over.

Griping at government and cops

Look It Up: You can tell by the names we give policemen that we don't always appreciate the authority they have. And yet the Bible says that Christians must obey and respect all civil authorities.

"Do you want to be free from fear of the one in authority? Then do what is right and he will commend you. For he is God's servant to do you good. But if you do wrong, be afraid, for he does not bear the sword for nothing. He is God's servant, an agent of wrath to bring punishment on the wrongdoer" (Romans 13:3-4).

Think It Through: Imagine what would happen if no civil authority existed.

We'd have no defense against foreign invasion. We'd have no system of justice to punish and therefore restrain criminals. People wouldn't bother to take you to court if they had a complaint against you. Instead, they'd just shoot you.

God has instituted civil government and declared rulers to be His servants (or ministers). We are to obey our rulers as His representatives unless they command us to do something God forbids, or forbid us to do something God commands (Acts 4:18-20).

Given those facts, if you unjustifiably rebel against government, against whom are you ultimately rebelling?

Work It Out: Thank God right now for civil authority that provides us with safety and security. The alternative is a land where people do whatever they want, whenever they want, to whomever they want.

Resolve to submit to civil authority by following all local, state, and federal regulations that apply to you. You'll please God and avoid a lot of trouble.

Nail It Down: Read 1 Peter 2:13-14.

Pray About It:

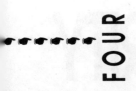

FOUR

65

Valerie works at a fast-food restaurant. It's not the greatest job in the world, but it is nice to have a couple hundred dollars of spending money each month.

The problem? Her boss is giving her the worst time slots and assigning her the grossest responsibilities. She just checked the weekend work schedule and saw that she was closing up both nights.

"Valerie," said her friend Melanie, "I'd tell him what he can do with his little schedule."

Don't forget who your real boss is!

Look It Up: Since slavery was a social institution during his time, Paul discussed principles for master-slave relations. Those same principles are applicable to Christians in today's workforce.

"Obey your earthly masters in everything; and do it, not only when their eye is on you and to win their favor, but with sincerity of heart and reverence for the Lord. Whatever you do, work at it with all your heart, as working for the Lord, not for men, since you know that you will receive an inheritance from the Lord as a reward. It is the Lord Christ you are serving" (Colossians 3:22-24).

Think It Through: Imagine the impact Christians could have if they committed themselves to serving their bosses with the same enthusiasm they put into serving God.

Do you realize that God is just as pleased with you when you flip hamburgers to His glory as He is when you sing to His glory in the church choir? We'll be rewarded for our attitude and effort in whatever workplace God places us in.

Work It Out: If you're employed as a clerk in a store, be the best clerk you can be. If you throw newspapers, do it as if Jesus Christ were your boss. If you baby-sit, do it with the single purpose of being excellent for the Lord.

Remember: The person who is working strictly for a paycheck has his reward. Work for Christ's kingdom wherever you are, and Christ will reward you (and you'll still get a paycheck).

Nail It Down: Read Ephesians 6:5-8. On Saturday, read Psalm 126:5-6. On Sunday, read Saturday's verses again. Have you ever worked so hard for something that you actually cried, only to rejoice when you finally got it?

FIVE AUTHORITY

PATIENCE

Even more than Aunt Rosie!

Whenever someone mentions God's patience, I often think back to my twelfth-grade calculus class. We had a student teacher: Miss Rosenboom. What a joke! She was four years older than we were, a college senior finishing up her required course work. No way were we gonna call her Miss. We finally settled on the nickname "Aunt Rosie."

We were awful. Singing in class. Laughing. Making obnoxious remarks. And always begging Aunt Rosie not to give us homework and tests.

Through all the shenanigans Aunt Rosie just kept quietly giving us "the look." How can I describe "the look"? It was a sly smile—an understanding sort of semi-grin in which her eyes would twinkle briefly, then crinkle shut. It was always followed by a movement in which our young instructor would turn and gaze out the window—looking forward, I'm sure, less to our graduation than to her own. In time, as silence would fall across the class, Aunt Rosie would again begin speaking softly.

Aunt Rosie put up with a lot during that semester. But an interesting thing happened by the end of those spring months.

Most of us had actually learned some calculus . . . and also had developed a deep admiration for a remarkable young woman named Miss Rosenboom. She was without question the most patient teacher I ever had. And certainly one of the most patient people I've ever known.

And the rest of the class? Well, at least two fellow seniors didn't get to graduate. They blamed Aunt Rosie for their failing math grades, but it wasn't her fault. No way.

Whether offering tutoring sessions after school, showing up at basketball games, or patiently flashing "the look," Miss Rosenboom was always there for us.

For me, the story of Miss Rosenboom is a good, though imperfect picture of how God patiently endures most of our stupid behavior. More than anything, He wants us to grasp, not calculus, but His care for us—the incredible love story of the gospel.

Abuse His patience by continuing to reject His love, and you'll suffer the painful consequences (Galatians 6:7). But take advantage of His patience, get to know Him, and you'll never regret it (2 Peter 3:9).

WORST
BIBLE JOKES

WARNING! These are unbelievably corny jokes! Only tell them if you want your friends to groan in disgust!

• Who were the shortest guys in the Bible?
Bildad the Shuhite (shoe height) in Job 2:11; Nehemiah (knee-high-miah) in the book bearing his name. And don't forget the Philippian jailer who fell asleep "on his watch" (Acts 16:27).

• Where is baseball mentioned in the Bible?
(Genesis 1:1) *"In the beginning . . ."* (The big inning, get it?)

• Where is tennis mentioned in the Bible?
(Esther 5:2) "When he saw Queen Esther standing in the court . . ."

• How did the people of Jericho feel after Joshua's armies left town?
They were crushed.

• Where is basketball mentioned in the Bible?
"Your basket . . . will be blessed" (Deuteronomy 28:5).

• What is the smallest sin in the Bible?
"Flee (flea) immorality . . . " (1 Corinthians 6:18 in the New American Standard Version of the Bible).

• What did Adam and Eve do after they got kicked out of the Garden of Eden?
They raised Cain.

• Who was the most wicked man in the Bible?
Moses. He broke all Ten Commandments at once (Exodus 32:19).

(Have you had enough yet? Only two more . . .)

• Besides Adam, who in the Bible had no parents?
Joshua was the son of Nun (Exodus 33:11).

• Why were the children of Israel sad when they came out of Egypt?
They had left their "mummies" behind.

(Aren't you glad that's finally over?)

RELATIONSHIPS
People: Social Creatures

R elationships. We can't live without them, and sometimes we can't live with them! This week let's explore our relationships in light of God's Word and find out how to

- make the most of our friendships with non-Christians;
- communicate in all our relationships;
- relate to our parents;
- deepen our relationship with God;
- make solid relationships even better.

"Be devoted to one another in brotherly love" (Romans 12:10).

As school is letting out, Lisa stops for a moment to tell Melinda she'll see her at youth group that evening.

"Is Kathy coming too?" Melinda asks.

"I doubt it. But I'm coming even if she doesn't."

Just then, Lisa hears Kathy's voice: "Lisa! Hey, a bunch of us are going over to Jeff's house tonight. His parents are out of town. Coming?"

"I don't think so, Kathy. I had planned to go to youth group."

"Oh, c'mon. It's not going to be that wild. We'll only stay a little while, I promise. Please?"

Friends are friends forever, right?

Look It Up: Lisa was glad she stuck to her guns and went to youth group that night. Believe it or not, her youth pastor spoke about friendship!

"We all have some non-Christian friends," he said. "How can we lead them to Christ and not allow ourselves to be led away from Christ?"

The youth pastor read 2 Corinthians 5:18-20: "God reconciled us to himself through Christ. . . . And he has committed to us the message of reconciliation. We are therefore Christ's ambassadors."

"You see," said Lisa's youth pastor, "we are God's representatives, sent to share with our non-Christian friends how Christ's death can make them acceptable to God. We have to be careful; we want to be ambassadors who make a difference in our non-Christian friends, not ambassadors who are made different by our non-Christian friends.

Think It Through: Think about your friends who don't know Christ. Are you, as God's ambassador, helping them to know the Lord? Or are they hurting and hindering your own walk with God?

Can you think of specific ways to be both a good friend and a good witness?

Work It Out: Introducing your non-Christian friends to Christ's friendship is a great privilege. Pray for strength to be a solid witness wherever you are.

Ask Christian friends to keep you in line as you seek to represent Christ to your friends who don't yet know Him.

Nail It Down: Read 1 Thessalonians 5:5-11.

ooooooooo ONE **RELATIONSHIPS**

A great friend has many friends

Melinda's thoughts: "Why isn't Lisa saying anything? She said she wanted to talk after youth group, but all we've done is drive around. If I ask her what's wrong, she'll think I'm being nosy. I wish I knew what to say."

Lisa's thoughts: "Maybe I shouldn't have asked Melinda to talk. I just didn't know what else to do. I know I need to be a better witness to Kathy and all my non-Christian friends. Melinda probably thinks I'm crazy just sitting here like this. But I'm afraid. What if she thinks I'm really bad for hanging around with Kathy?"

Look It Up: Why is it so hard to take risks? Because we're afraid we'll be laughed at or misunderstood if we share our deepest thoughts.

God has a better idea for relationships: "An anxious heart weighs a man down, but a kind word cheers him up" (Proverbs 12:25).

In other words, communication (and that includes both talking and listening) is crucial to meaningful friendships. When good friends communicate, they should be truthful and tender, "speaking the truth in love" (Ephesians 4:15).

Think It Through: Are your friendships marked by close, caring communication? Do you have friends you can share your deepest feelings with?

Since we have two ears and only one mouth, maybe we ought to listen twice as much as we talk! Consider how well you listen to others. Are you sensitive to what's going on inside your friends? If you sense they want to talk, do you help draw them out? Or do you just clam up, thinking it's not worth the risk?

Work It Out: When your friends are hurting, let them know you care. Gently ask what's wrong. Listen, but don't force them to talk. You'll make more real friends by becoming interested in others than by trying to get others interested in you. Make sure your words are truthful and tender.

If, on the other hand, you're the one who's hurting, find a true friend and be vulnerable. As you open yourself to others you can trust, you'll see your friendships deepen and grow as never before.

Nail It Down: Read Proverbs 16:24; 1 Thessalonians 5:14.

Pray About It: _____

TWO

○○○○○○○

71

"Brian! How many times have I told you to pick up your coat! Why do I have to tell you a thousand times to do the simplest things!"

"Sorry, Mom—"

"Where have you been all afternoon, young man?"

"Uh, practice went late today, and then I had to go to the bookstore to—"

"Brian, why can't you just do a simple thing like come home when you're supposed to? I don't like you running all over the place. I'm sick of it!"

Home sweet (and sour) home

Look It Up: More than any other human relationship, your relationship with your parents affects the rest of your life.

God has given parents a five-part "job description" when it comes to their kids:
- protect them (Hebrews 11:23);
- train them (Deuteronomy 6:6-7);
- provide for them (2 Corinthians 12:14);
- nurture them toward maturity (Genesis 18:19); and
- correct them (Hebrews 12:8-10).

Now that's no easy job!

How are we supposed to respond to our parents? "Children, obey your parents in the Lord, for this is right" (Ephesians 6:1).

Sure, it's not easy. But it's possible, in the power of the Spirit, to obey God's commands.

Think It Through: When you run up against your parents, ask yourself, "Why are they acting this way? Have I done something wrong, or are they just tired? Am I reacting in the right way, or maybe making things worse?"

There are two sides to every issue. You want them to trust and respect you; that means you have to trust them and be worthy of their trust and respect.

Work It Out: What would you do if you were Brian in the story? How could you get your mom to listen?

Here's a thought: After dinner, ask her how her day went. Listen to her. Then gently say something like this: "Mom, I want to explain why I was late today. Please listen to what I have to say." Showing respect by obeying your parents always makes for a milder climate at home. And it can pave the way for a closer relationship.

Nail It Down: Read Proverbs 3:11-12; Hebrews 12:8-11.

THREE **RELATIONSHIPS**

Rob's friends know something is different about Rob. Sure he has problems, but he seems to know how to handle them. How does he do it? Every morning, Rob goes to a special place—a bay window overlooking the backyard. He sits by that window, opens his Bible, and spends some time thinking about what he reads.

Like Moses, who talked face to face with God and received strength to lead millions of Israelites, Rob has discovered that a close relationship with God is not only possible, but it results in a powerful life.

He's the best friend I have

Look It Up: Moses' relationship with God is described in Exodus 33:8-11. God called David a "man after his own heart" (1 Samuel 13:14). Abraham "was called God's friend" (James 2:23).

But friendship with God isn't something only people in the Bible could enjoy: "Greater love has no one than this, that he lay down his life for his friends. You are my friends if you do what I command" (John 15:13-14).

Imagine being able to call the Creator-God of all the universe your personal Friend!

Think It Through: How do we become God's friend? We must trust in Christ alone, seeing His death as the only acceptable payment for our sins (Ephesians 2:8-9). When we put our trust in Christ, we become His friend.

But like any friendship, our relationship with God needs to grow. So how do we deepen an existing friendship with God? By communicating with Him. God speaks to us through the Bible. We speak to Him through prayer.

Work It Out: If you've never trusted Christ as your Savior, you can do so right now and begin to experience an exciting friendship with God.

If you've already trusted Christ but would like to grow in that relationship, do what Rob did. Agree to meet with the Lord for at least 10 minutes of prayer and Bible reading each morning—try it for one week. Ask God to deepen your relationship with Him in the process.

That's a request He will grant!

Nail It Down: Read Ephesians 1:15-19; 3:14-19.

Pray About It:

FOUR
OOOOOOO

73

Jennifer JeJeune is a real "friend." She
- always puts you down;
- always argues with you;
- always gripes;
- always whines;
- is constantly negative;
- never listens;
- blabs your most intimate secrets;
- borrows but never repays;
- lies about everything;
- cares about nothing but herself.

Do you have any so-called friends like Jennifer?

Factors in fantastic relationships

Look It Up: Real friends make a difference in the way you get through life.

Here are seven key qualities of real friends:

1. Commitment—promising you'll work at being friends, no matter what. "A man of many companions may come to ruin, but there is a friend who sticks closer than a brother" (Proverbs 18:24).

2. Respect—acknowledging each other as children of God, and therefore persons of worth and importance. "Show proper respect to everyone" (1 Peter 2:17).

3. Communication—talking to one another about your struggles, dreams, fears. "The pleasantness of one's friend springs from his earnest counsel" (Proverbs 27:9).

4. Trust—keeping secrets. "A trustworthy man keeps a secret" (Proverbs 11:13).

5. Honesty—"Wounds from a friend can be trusted" (Proverbs 27:6). If a true friend tells you something in love and it hurts, he's only doing it to help you.

6. Self-giving—putting the other person first by sacrificing your time and energy. "Do nothing out of selfish ambition or vain conceit, but in humility consider others better than yourselves" (Philippians 2:3).

7. Brotherly love—the bottom line. "Be devoted to one another in brotherly love" (Romans 12:10).

Think It Through and Work It Out: Reflect on these seven factors. Grade yourself in each area. Then pick one or two of the areas you're weakest in. Ask God to change you, and ask a friend to hold you accountable once a week for the next two months by giving you an honest progress report.

Nail It Down: 1 John 4:7-21. On Saturday, read the same passage again, and on Sunday, read it a third time. Get the point?

FIVE RELATIONSHIPS

74

SIN

Seeing Through the Big Lie

Hundreds of times a day Mr. Temptation, the world's greatest salesman, knocks on your door. He sells every kind of sin you can imagine, and if you listen too long, his sales pitch will convince you to buy. The problem is, he doesn't deliver the goods. You never quite get what you were hoping for.

Examine the scam of sin with us this week—where it came from and what it does to us.

Learn to slam the door right in Mr. Temptation's face.

"If you do what is right, will you not be accepted? But if you do not do what is right, sin is crouching at your door; it desires to have you, but you must master it" (Genesis 4:7).

The 150 teens were quiet as the camp speaker discussed sin.

"The Bible says sin is everything about us that fails to measure up to God's perfect character. It may be outrageous acts—setting your school on fire, selling drugs, or killing someone.

"But more often we sin through simple acts—a white lie, a put-down, picking on our kid brother.

"And it's not just outer actions. It's also attitudes: bitterness, lusting, thinking we're better than someone.

"Hey, whether it's our thoughts or actions, we all are guilty of sin."

Evil in the Garden of Eden

Look It Up: The Bible says this about sin:
"All have sinned and fall short of the glory of God" (Romans 3:23).

"Through the disobedience of the one man the many were made sinners" (Romans 5:19). This verse refers to the sinful nature we inherited from Adam.

When Adam decided that he knew better than God what was right and what was wrong, he plunged all of his descendants (the whole human race) into sin. At that moment, ugliness and alienation shattered the perfection and beauty of life with God in Eden.

Think It Through: How can one man's sin long, long, ago affect us at the end of the 20th century? Do we really have Adam's sinful nature?

Imagine a jello mold. It makes the same shape every time, right? Now, what if you dropped and dented it? From that point on, every salad produced by the mold would be dented—marred by the mold's imperfection.

In the same way, once Adam and Eve sinned, they could only produce sinful offspring, who could only produce sinful offspring, and so on. We aren't sinners because we sin. We sin because we are, by nature, sinful.

Work It Out: If this prayer expresses how you feel, pray it (or something like it) to God: "Lord, I know that I do things I shouldn't, and don't do things I should. I'm sorry. Teach me about sin this week as I examine what Your Word says. Thank You for Jesus. Help me to obey You more this week, for Christ's sake. Amen."

Nail It Down: Read about the worst moment in human history: Genesis 3. How often do you, like Adam, decide for yourself what is right and what is wrong?

▼▼▼▼▼▼▼▼ ONE SIN ▼▼▼▼▼▼▼▼▼▼▼▼▼▼

Nikki and Chad had one of the best weeks of their lives at camp. Not only did they meet each other, but they both really grew spiritually.

How are they doing now that they're back home? Not too well. You see, last night they went "all the way."

Chad laments, "I never meant for it to happen. We'd go to Nikki's every day after school—and just goof off. And, well . . . nobody was ever around. One thing just led to another, and before we knew it . . . "

Temptation's tantalizing trap

Look It Up: Sin can sneak up on you.

"Each one is tempted when, by his own evil desire, he is dragged away and enticed. Then, after desire has conceived, it gives birth to sin; and sin, when it is full-grown, gives birth to death" (James 1:14-15).

Nikki and Chad saw the bait of sexual sin . . . and got hooked.

Think It Through: The story of King David illustrates this principle. While strolling on his rooftop, he looked too long at a bathing beauty. Strike one.

Without really thinking, he sent a messenger to find out about her. Strike two.

Then, this king sent for the woman and slept with her. Strike three—you're out, David! (See 2 Samuel 11:1-5.)

Sexual desire is a God-given emotion, and therefore, not in-and-of-itself sinful. But acting on that desire is most certainly sinful if it's done outside the moral boundaries clearly set in God's Word.

Question: Where does God's Word draw those moral boundaries? In other words, when is it morally acceptable to act on your sexual desire?

Answer: When you're married to a person of the opposite sex. Period!

Work It Out: Remember: Temptation doesn't just occur with sexual sin. People lust for all sorts of things—food, drink, money, power, and the possessions of others.

At school today, look for this principle at work. Watch how people (including you) deal with various temptations. Note the consequences when they fail.

Finally, take courage. If you really want to escape the temptation trap, you can. God always leaves an out.

Nail It Down: Read 1 Corinthians 10:13.

Pray About It:

▼▼▼▼▼▼ TWO

In the last few months Nikki and Chad have continued to have sex. Recently they broke up for good. How has all this affected them?

Nikki: "At first, I felt so close to Chad, but after a while we quit talking. We'd get together and immediately start kissing. It's like your mind says, 'No!' but your body says, 'Go!' Now I feel scared and ... well, dirty.

"I guess it just wasn't what I expected—and I really miss Chad."

Chad: "I knew better, but I was so curious. I know this much—sex isn't worth feeling so far away from God."

You don't get what you pay for

Look It Up: The awful consequences of sin.

Adam and Eve were the first to learn this lesson. After disobeying God, they tried to hide. When God called out to them, Adam said, "I heard you in the garden, and I was afraid because I was naked; so I hid" (Genesis 3:10).

Feelings of fear, shame (at their nakedness), and guilt (revealed in their hiding) all followed their disobedience.

But the worst consequence of sin wasn't guilt feelings; it was real guilt—guilt before the judgment seat of God. And even though God graciously provided Adam and Eve with the hope of a Savior, He drove them from His presence with a curse (Genesis 3:17-24).

Think It Through: Consider Nikki and Chad. Both of them feel guilty. Does feeling guilty after sinning eliminate all of sin's consequences? Did Adam and Eve's guilt feelings eliminate all of the consequences of their sin?

Not a chance! In fact, you, your parents, your friends, everyone on this planet is still suffering the consequences of the sin of our first parents.

The point? Don't kid yourself! Sin, even confessed and forgiven sin, has consequences.

Work It Out: List some possible consequences of these situations:
- going out drinking with friends
- cheating in school
- watching dirty movies on cable
- having a loose tongue

Ask God to give you a hatred for sin, the wisdom to see the consequences of a sinful lifestyle, and the grace to say no to temptation.

Nail It Down: Memorize Romans 12:9.

THREE SIN

Chad and Nikki quit going out about seven weeks ago, and gradually they're getting back on track with God.

Nikki discusses her struggle: "At first the hardest part was missing Chad. We had so much fun together, and he was like my best friend. Then I felt so far away from God . . . like He hated me for what I'd done. I bet I looked up every verse in the whole Bible on forgiveness 100 times. I'd give anything to go back and do things differently, but I can't. Sometimes I don't feel forgiven. But if the Bible's really true, I have to believe I am."

Wiping the slate clean

Look It Up: Here's one of the verses Nikki found:

"In him we have redemption through his blood, the forgiveness of sins, in accordance with the riches of God's grace" (Ephesians 1:7).

This passage became even more special to her when she realized it was written by a man who had earlier tried to crush Christianity—he even favored the murder of Christian leaders!

But this enemy of Christ met the Lord on the road to Damascus. And not only did Christ completely forgive him, he also used him to change the world.

If God can forgive Paul, he can forgive Nikki, Chad, and you.

Think It Through: Can you remember ever feeling like Nikki? You knew in your head that God said you were forgiven, but you didn't feel it in your heart?

Choose the option you think is more trustworthy:
- You and your fickle feelings
- God and His enduring Word

No contest, is it?

Work It Out: Do something unusual: Read the Ten Commandments (Exodus 20:1-21). After you've done that,

1. Confess those areas in which you've been rebelling against God and doing your own thing. Agree with God that His judgments are right, yours are wrong.

2. Humbly repent of those sins and ask God to wash you clean of them.

3. Just as you've agreed with God about sin, agree with Him about forgiveness. Trust Him when He says that all who truly confess their sins are forgiven.

Nail It Down: Read 1 John 1:9-10.

Pray About It: ────────────────

F O U R

79

Chad and Nikki have struggled to put the past behind them. She's been spending time with God every day and feels stronger spiritually. He's on the verge of blowing it again with his new girlfriend, Missy.

Chad: "We haven't gotten too carried away yet. But if things keep on, it'll be trouble. It scares me too, because I remember how bad I felt before . . . and for such a long time. Doesn't the Bible say that Christians won't be tempted?"

Telling temptation to take a hike

Look It Up: As long as we live in this world, we'll constantly face temptation. But that doesn't mean we have to yield.

Want to make temptation scram? Ask God to change your desires. King David didn't trust in himself; he trusted God to work inside him. "Create in me a pure heart, O God, and renew a steadfast spirit within me" (Psalm 51:10).

What's more, do your part by avoiding tempting situations. Joseph literally ran when Potiphar's wife tried to seduce him (Genesis 39:1-12).

Paul wrote, "Flee the evil desires of youth, and pursue righteousness, faith, love and peace, along with those who call on the Lord out of a pure heart" (2 Timothy 2:22).

Think It Through: Why do you think it's important to ask God to change your heart—your thoughts and desires? How do you think God can give you that new perspective? (Hint: See Romans 12:2.)

Why is it important to physically avoid tempting situations? Or, put another way, what would happen to an alcoholic who was trying to quit drinking if he hung out in bars every night? How smart would it be for a guy who was trying to overcome his lust problem to watch "soft porn" movies on cable?

Work It Out: List the sins that trip you up the most. Now, ask God to work in your life so that you no longer have the desire to do those things. It won't happen overnight, but if you're serious about renewing your mind by studying His Word and if you're faithful in your prayer, God will begin to radically change your life.

Nail It Down: Read 1 Corinthians 10:13 (again). Spend time on Saturday and Sunday memorizing that verse.

▼▼▼▼▼▼▼ FIVE **SIN** ▼▼▼▼▼▼▼▼▼▼▼▼▼

ATTITUDES
From Badness to Gladness

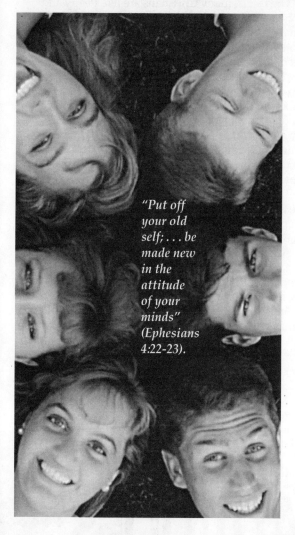

"Put off your old self; . . . be made new in the attitude of your minds" (Ephesians 4:22-23).

Hey, you're a teenager. You're supposed to be having fun, right? Then why are so many people (including Christians) acting like jerks? Why do bad attitudes infect so many teenage brains and ruin the fun and the friendships?

It doesn't have to be that way. You can receive a new outlook this week. And that gift is far more valuable and more lasting than any car, stereo, or new clothes.

Turn the page for some thoughts on how to turn a bad *attitude* into *gratitude.*

"I've got it!" Paul shouted. "Instead of just talking about abortion being wrong, let's do something!

"We can have a weekend flea market in the church parking lot to raise funds for the crisis pregnancy center. We'll get everyone to donate stuff. It'll be great!"

Peggy and Robyn stared at Paul like he was a moron. Finally Peggy spoke up. "Paul, look. Something like that would take a lot of work. Besides, I'm sure some other church is already doing something."

Robyn sighed, "Yeah. Maybe some other time."

Apathy: "Who cares?"

Look It Up: Paul is sympathetic toward the unborn. The girls are apathetic. Paul is interested in meeting needs. The girls are indifferent.

The fact is, many Christians are like Peggy and Robyn. They have lost the desire to serve God. They have become lazy and uninterested in helping others. Notice what the Lord told the apathetic believers who lived in Ephesus:

"I hold this against you: You have forsaken your first love. Remember the height from which you have fallen! Repent and do the things you did at first" (Revelation 2:4-5).

Think It Through: Ever had this experience? You're excited about the Lord and living for Him when—wham! The warm feelings suddenly fizzle.

That's not bad or wrong. Feelings come and go all the time. What's bad is when we let those blah feelings keep us from doing what's right. That's apathy. And God hates it (Isaiah 32:9; Amos 6:1).

Are you apathetic about your walk with God?

Work It Out: The key to overcoming the attitude of apathy is not by trying to crank up a bunch of ooey-gooey feelings. Your response should be to "repent and do the things you did at first." That means no matter how you feel, you need to do these things today and every day:

• Talk to God in prayer (Ephesians 6:18).
• Listen to God speak by reading His Word (Acts 20:32).
• Show love to fellow believers (Ephesians 1:15).
• Reach out to non-Christians (Ephesians 2:1-10).

In other words, the best weapon against apathy is action!

Nail It Down: Read Luke 12:47-48.

ONE ATTITUDES

So here's what I was thinking we could do, Randy. I mean, we've got to do something for the crisis pregnancy center in the neighborhood. So we could have this huge flea market in the church parking lot in two weeks. We could call it 'The World's for Sale' and really promote it!"

Randy looked shocked. "Paul, we're supposed to go surfing that weekend! C'mon, dude, priorities!"

"We do that all the time. Besides, this is a chance to really do something to help protect unborn children."

"If you ask me," Chris said, "I vote for the surfing."

Selfishness: "What do I get out of it?"

Look It Up: No one has to teach us to think about ourselves. That attitude comes naturally. As Christians, however, we are responsible to (and are able to) exhibit a supernatural, other-centered attitude.

"Do nothing out of selfish ambition or vain conceit, but in humility consider others better than yourselves. Each of you should look not only to your own interests, but also to the interests of others.

"Your attitude should be the same as that of Christ Jesus: Who, being in very nature God, did not consider equality with God something to be grasped, but made himself nothing. . . . He humbled himself and became obedient to death" (Philippians 2:3-8).

Think It Through: Why do health clubs cover their walls with mirrors? Why is it that when somebody hands us pictures we always look first to see which ones we're in?

Put yourself in the situation above. What should Paul's group do? What do you think you would do?

Work It Out: Selfish attitudes don't have to rule your life. You can, by the power and grace of God, be different.

First, pray: "Dear God, I know I am selfish at times. I don't want to be like that. Please change me. Cause me to think less of myself and more about others today. Make me aware of their feelings and needs, and show me creative ways to put them first, just as Christ did. Amen."

Second, think of one unselfish act that you can do for a family member or friend and do it. Lend a hand, give your time, share a possession, help with a problem. Unselfishness is costly, but it fulfills like nothing else!

Nail It Down: Read 2 Timothy 3:1-2.

Pray About It:

T W O

"The World's for Sale" is in full swing. The church parking lot is filled with clothing, toys, furniture, records, books, and customers. There's even a Christian band playing to attract passers-by.

Check out Linda Bray's thoughts as Mitzi Cooper leads the band in a rendition of "El Shaddai":

"That Mitzi . . . I can't stand her! I mean, she's so perfect. Great voice. Great body. Perfect skin. It's disgusting. Look at all the guys smiling at her. Why can't I be like that?"

Envy: "I want what you've got"

Look It Up: Here's how envy works. We see that someone else has a trait or possession that we don't have. Then, rather than appreciating that person's gifts and abilities we begin to compare. Quickly we end up resentful of the other person's good fortune and dissatisfied with our own situation.

Question: How do you think God feels about envy?

Answer: Read these verses to find out:

• "Love . . . does not envy" (1 Corinthians 13:4).

• "Let us not become conceited, provoking and envying each other" (Galatians 5:26).

Think It Through: The first verse comes from a passage that defines what love is by describing what it does . . . and what it doesn't do.

The second verse directs us not to be envious. But the question is how. It's easy to say, "Don't be envious," but how are we to experience victory when powerful feelings of envy overcome us?

The answer is found in Galatians 5:16-25. Can you see what it is?

Work It Out: The only way to defeat the attitude of envy is by living under the control of the Holy Spirit. If you are envious of someone, you can take these steps right now:

1. Admit the sin of envy and ask God to root it out of your life (Galatians 5:19-21).

2. Surrender the control of your life to the Holy Spirit. Ask God to cultivate spiritual fruit in your life (Galatians 5:22).

3. Remember frequently that envy (and every other wrong passion and desire) was defeated at the Cross. Envy can only control us if we allow it to (Galatians 5:24).

Nail It Down: Read Proverbs 14:30.

THREE ATTITUDES

Paul's youth pastor let out a whoop. He had just finished counting the money raised at "The World's for Sale" for the crisis pregnancy center. He couldn't believe the figure: over $8,000!

Monte saw things differently: "Did you see how many black and Hispanic people were there?" he whispered to his friend Kevin. "I didn't like seeing them on our church parking lot. I hope we never do anything like that again."

Prejudice: "I don't like difference"

Look It Up: How are we to react to those who are different from us? By building walls of suspicion and hostility? By name calling? No! As followers of Christ, we must tear down walls and build bridges.

Look what happened when Jesus encountered a Samaritan woman. Cultural prejudice demanded that Jesus, a male, Jewish religious leader ignore this Samaritan woman who was involved in adultery.

When Jesus began talking with the woman, she replied, " 'You are a Jew and I am a Samaritan woman. How can you ask me for a drink?' (For Jews do not associate with Samaritans.)" (John 4:9).

In the end, Jesus' refusal to let unjustified bigotry cloud His thinking led to the salvation of the woman and many of her townspeople (John 4:39-42).

Think It Through: Prejudice is the irrational prejudging of either individuals or groups of people. Racial prejudice is prejudging solely on the basis of someone's belonging to a particular race or ethnic group.

Is prejudice between different groups present at your school? In your own life?

Work It Out: Break down the ugly walls of prejudice by reaching out to someone you consider different —a punker, a preppie, a jock, a brain, a nerd, someone of a different race. A good way to start is to remember that we're all sinners who need Christ.

How do you break the ice? Begin a conversation. Ask the person to help you out. That's what Jesus did. By causing people to feel needed and accepted, we build bridges. And that's when God begins to change lives!

Nail It Down: Read Acts 10:28.

Pray About It: ——————

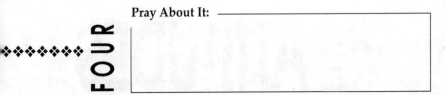

✦✦✦✦✦✦✦ FOUR

85

After the highly successful parking lot sale, everyone is praising Paul for thinking of such a wonderful idea. Suddenly he's feeling quite saintly. Here are some of his thoughts:

• When Chris told him about surfing, Paul thought, "When are you going to cut out the self-centered activities and start doing things for others?"

• When Paul's youth pastor praised him as an example of a Christian really living out his faith, Paul thought, "You know, if you'd let me help with planning the group's activities, we could turn this community upside down for Christ."

"Compared to the rest, I'm the best."

Look It Up: Pride is the craftiest of all bad attitudes. By making us think we're better than others, it sneaks in even when we're trying to do what's right.

Pride is also the deadliest of all bad attitudes. It brings
• disgrace—"When pride comes, then comes disgrace, but with humility comes wisdom" (Proverbs 11:2);
• destruction—"Pride goes before destruction, a haughty spirit before a fall" (Proverbs 16:18). It was pride that caused Lucifer, the noblest and highest of angels, to sin. When he did so, he became Satan, the prince of demons (Isaiah 14:12-15).

Think It Through: C. S. Lewis has wisely observed about pride, "Whenever we find that our religious life is making us feel that we are good—above all, that we are better than someone else—I think we may be sure that we are being acted on, not by God, but by the devil."

Question: Are proud, supersaint attitudes common in your life?

Work It Out: Do two things today to keep pride from gaining a foothold in your life.

First, check your beliefs. Don't get cocky; instead, see yourself as you really are (Romans 12:3). Remember that apart from Christ you can do nothing (John 15:5).

Second, check your behavior. Don't rush to be in the spotlight. Be willing to serve humbly in the background. If God does exalt you, don't grab the glory that belongs to Him (Acts 12:21-23).

God wants you to do your best. He just wants you to remember who you are: a sinner saved by grace.

Nail It Down: Read Luke 18:9-14. On Saturday, check out the Apostle Paul's attitude—1 Timothy 1:15. On Sunday, read 1 Timothy 1:16.

FIVE ATTITUDES

MATERIALISM

We live, as one pop singer put it, in a material world. We are constantly confronted with new items and are told, "You've got to have this." Deep down we think, "If only I could (drive this car, wear those clothes, have that gadget, live in such-and-such a house—take your pick), then I'd be happy." We think and act as though material goods will bring us the satisfaction we long for in life.

Is this the way believers in Christ should live? What does God say about material possessions?

Material wealth in the Bible. By scanning the pages of Scripture, we find that material possessions are often the result of hard work (Proverbs 12:27). However, Paul carefully pointed out that *"we brought nothing into the world, and we can take nothing out of it"* (1 Timothy 6:7). So, no matter how many possessions we might accumulate we can't take them with us when we die. (That's why you've never seen a hearse pulling a U-Haul to the graveyard!)

Jesus and materialism. Jesus told His followers to store up treasures in heaven, rather than treasure on earth. His reasoning was clear—worldly wealth is temporal. At worst it can be destroyed or stolen; at best it will decay. By contrast, heavenly treasure is eternal (Matthew 6:19-21) and can never be lost.

Jesus understood that what we value in life will determine our direction in life. When we value earthly things and invest in them, our focus is on the material world. On the other hand, when we concentrate our time, energy, and resources on eternal investments, we are more concerned with the things of God.

So what? Having material goods is not wrong. Some are very necessary to life. However, when we make the accumulation of material things our primary goal in life, we have a problem. We are guilty of idolatry.

As a follower of Christ . . .

• What possessions matter most to you?

• How would you react if you lost those possessions?

• Are you investing in what can be lost or in what will always last?

"For where your treasure is, there your heart will be also" (Matthew 6:21).

No Halfdom in the Kingdom

Think about this: What good is . . .

. . . *half a night out with friends?* ("Oops! Nine o'clock—gotta get home!")

. . . *half a perfect score on a test?* ("Look class! Thelma made a 50 on her quiz!")

. . . *half a TV show?* ("We interrupt this program to bring you live coverage of the City Council zoning meeting.")

. . . *half a birthday gift?* ("Here's the CD player you wanted. You'll get the speakers next year.")

. . . *half a kiss* ("Only one lip, please.")

. . . *half a paycheck?* ("You worked hard, Spike—here's your half-pay. We're keeping the other half.")

Not much you say? You're right. So why do we often give God only *half* a heart?

You want all, not just half, right? Well, guess what? God feels exactly the same way (Revelation 3:15-16).

It's pretty easy to be a "half Christian"—thinking about God every now and then, being committed only when you "feel" like it, living for Him just when you're around the people from church.

But the result? A half-abundant, half-fulfilling life. And that's a real drag. After all, half of nothing is . . . nothing. So give God your whole life. If you've never trusted Christ to forgive your sins and give you His eternal life, you need to do that right now. Ask Him to come in and change your life.

If you're a Christian with a halfway commitment, you need to re-evaluate your priorities. Turn over your plans and wishes and dreams to Him. Determine to follow Him 100 percent of the time, in every situation . . . and then watch Him in return give you all the blessings He has for you.

ALCOHOL
The Straight Scoop

Alcohol—the drug of choice for high school students.
If the latest statistics are correct, at least one out of every three high school seniors will get loaded this weekend. About five million teenagers are problem drinkers.

Given the terrible problems of alcohol-related teen deaths in automobile accidents and by suicide, this is a subject we need to confront.

Join us this week as we explore the Bible for the truth about teens and the bottle.

"Do not get drunk on wine, which leads to debauchery. Instead be filled with the Spirit" (Ephesians 5:18).

Last weekend, Mary, 16, went to a party at a friend's house. A couple of guys had mixed up a cooler of vodka and lemonade. Soon everyone was trashed. Mary can't remember how she got home, she has a headache to end all headaches, and the mess in her room is just too gross.

• Jason, 17, left a party drunk, crashed his car, and seriously injured the friend who was with him. He was arrested for DUI and has to appear in court. He may lose his license and will be fined and sentenced to do community work.

Devastating dangers of drink

Look It Up: Research findings have scientifically confirmed what has long been suspected: Alcohol abuse is both physically and psychologically devastating. God's Word has contained this information for centuries.

"Who has woe? Who has sorrow? Who has strife? Who has complaints? Who has needless bruises? Who has bloodshot eyes? Those who linger over wine, who go to sample bowls of mixed wine. Do not gaze at wine when it is red, when it sparkles in the cup, when it goes down smoothly! In the end it bites like a snake and poisons like a viper. Your eyes will see strange sights and your mind imagine confusing things. . . . You will say, . . . 'When will I wake up so I can find another drink?' " (Proverbs 23:29-35).

Think It Through: The commercials on television and the ads in magazines don't tell the full story. They always show beautiful people laughing, smiling, and looking cool. They don't show the people who wind up red-faced and on their knees, hugging the toilet.

How come we don't ever see the people who end up in some chemical dependency unit, crying their eyes out because of the way they wrecked their lives? Why don't we see those who suffer from liver and/or brain damage?

Work It Out: Call your local chapter of Alcoholics Anonymous. Find out when their next meeting is. Then grab a friend and go. You don't have to say anything. Just sit and watch. It will be an evening you won't forget.

Also, stop by the library and ask the librarian for copies of articles on teens and alcohol in magazines like *Time* and *Newsweek*.

Nail It Down: Read Proverbs 23:19-21.

| | | ONE ALCOHOL |

R eggie, 16, has something he'd like to say:

"I'm sick and tired of all the sermons about not drinking. As long as you don't get ripped every weekend, as long as you don't drive under the influence, as long as you can handle it, it's just not that big a deal. Show me a verse in the Bible that says, 'Don't drink.' You can't because there isn't one. It says, 'Don't get drunk.' I don't usually get drunk, so get off my back."

The bottom line on boozing it up

Look It Up: Let's grant Reggie his point: The Bible doesn't specifically state, "Don't drink." But the Bible does speak directly to some relevant issues.

• Drinking can quickly lead to drunkenness. The Apostle Paul wrote, "Do not get drunk on wine, which leads to debauchery. Instead, be filled with the Spirit" (Ephesians 5:18).

• Since Reggie is under-age, his drinking is illegal. Christians are commanded to obey the civil authorities.

"Everyone must submit himself to the governing authorities. . . . The authorities that exist have been established by God. Consequently, he who rebels against the authority is rebelling against what God has instituted, and those who do so will bring judgment on themselves" (Romans 13:1-2).

Think It Through: Sincere and thoughtful Christians differ on whether alcohol is ever permissible for adults.

But Christians do not differ on this: For an underage party animal to slam down a 12-pack at a wild, "parentless" bash is immoral. According to God's Word, if people engage in such rebellious, illegal behavior, they will eventually "bring judgment" on themselves.

Work It Out: If you're underage, no other argument is needed. If drinking is illegal for you, it's immoral for you. Period.

This weekend, have an alternative party with some friends. Pick a word or phrase for your theme. Then plan some ridiculous games, strange food, and appropriate music to go along. You may discover that it's possible to have weekend fun without a beer run!

Nail It Down: Read 1 Corinthians 10:32-11:1.

Pray About It: ─────────────────────

T W O

Albert, 14, is new in town. He got drunk with some guys in his neighborhood last Saturday because he wants them to like and accept him.

• Marie, 18, has demanding parents who expect their children to go to top-notch colleges and become as successful as they are. Because Marie can't cope with that pressure, she drinks . . . a lot.

• Emmitt, 15, lives in an inner-city neighborhood. He only goes to school to play sports. But if Emmitt keeps drinking, he'll never make it to the pros. He's practically a wino.

The emptiness of an empty bottle

Look It Up: Only Jesus can meet our deepest needs.

Do teens drink to be liked and accepted? Jesus accepts you for who you are, not on the basis of how quickly you can down a six-pack (1 John 4:10).

Are teens afraid of failure? "So do not fear, for I am with you; do not be dismayed, for I am your God. I will strengthen you and help you" (Isaiah 41:10).

Do teens drink to escape the problems of life? People don't have to run away from difficulties (Psalm 23:4).

Do teens try to drown their disappointments in alcohol? They don't have to. They have a comforting companion in the Lord (2 Corinthians 1:3-4).

Think It Through: Beer commercials and liquor ads are sneaky. They're designed to communicate the idea that if you party down with their product, you'll have friends, be funny, end up hanging out with all the right people, and be the life of the party like Spuds McKenzie. However, you're more likely to drool in public, lose friends, act stupid, end up with the wrong crowd, and be a dud instead of ole Spuds.

Work It Out: Watch television until you see at least three alcohol commercials. Evaluate each one. What are they really saying? Do you honestly believe that message?

Then for the rest of the week (or at least until your parents tell you to shut up), yell at the television every time a misleading commercial for alcohol comes on. Here are some suggested phrases: "Oh, sure!" "Yeah right!" or "Who are you trying to kid?"

Remember: Jesus, not alcohol, is the answer to the problems you face. Spend some time getting to know Him better today.

Nail It Down: Read 1 Peter 5:7.

IIIIIIIIII THREE **ALCOHOL** IIII

Amy went to a New Year's Eve party where there was a lot of alcohol. Though she had never taken a drink before, she was curious. She drank a beer. Then a shot of tequila. It tasted awful, but she felt great. She laughed and felt less inhibited. And people seemed to accept her.

Amy thought she had found a new way to overcome her feelings of inferiority. Soon, each weekend was the same story—partying and getting tanked. Now, two years later, Amy has a serious problem: she's an alcoholic.

Hi, I'm Amy. I'm an alcoholic.

Look It Up: The Bible is full of stories about people who found help in God. King David is one example.

Badgered by Saul, bushwhacked by his own sin, and betrayed by his son Absalom, David knew how it feels to be in trouble. Listen to his prayer in Psalm 6:

"Be merciful to me, LORD, for I am faint; O LORD, heal me, for my bones are in agony. My soul is in anguish. How long, O LORD, how long?" (vv. 2-4).

Soon David receives the comfort and peace he needs. He goes on to say, "The LORD has heard my cry for mercy; the LORD accepts my prayer" (v. 9).

Think It Through: As far as we know, David—though he faced all sorts of problems—never struggled with alcohol. Big deal. When you're in trouble, the issue isn't your problem. It's finding a solution.

If God loves and is willing to help prostitutes (John 8:1-11), diseased individuals (Matthew 8:1-3), and criminals (Luke 23:39-43), don't you think He has room in His heart for alcoholics?

Work It Out: Can you relate to Amy? Do you have a drinking problem too? The first (and perhaps hardest) step is to admit you need help. Pour out your feelings to God. By saying, "I can't control my drinking," you take a giant step toward wholeness. Second, find an older person you trust and tell him or her about your situation.

If you have friends like Amy, begin praying for them. Then look for opportunities to confront them about their drinking. Be gentle and loving, but firm. Tell them that you care and are willing to go the distance with them.

In either case, don't wait. Now is the time for action.

Nail It Down: Read Psalm 38.

Pray About It:

IIIIIIII FOUR

93

Here's the mask Lynne wears: outgoing, fun-loving, and active. But on the inside she feels lonely, fearful, and inferior.

When people look at Evan they see a smart, hardworking, all-American kid. Evan sees himself as a useless failure.

Karen is quiet and usually keeps to herself. But every now and then she explodes with anger. Classmates avoid her, saying, "She's psycho!"

Lynne, Evan, and Karen all live with alcoholic parents.

They have learned to cope with their worlds by not talking, trusting, or feeling.

Surviving the hell of an alcoholic home

Look It Up: It's easy to see why the children of alcoholics react the way they do. But by clamming up, retreating, and burying their feelings, they prolong the pain and the problem.

Children of alcoholics need to talk—to God (Philippians 4:6-7) and to friends (Proverbs 12:25; Galatians 6:2).

Children of alcoholics need to trust. Just because a parent has proven to be unreliable doesn't mean everyone else is untrustworthy. God is 100 percent dependable. Children of alcoholics need to express their emotions. King David was a man of intense emotion—joy, anger, sadness, depression—and an expressive man.

Think It Through: Is the child of an alcoholic responsible for his parent's problem? NO WAY!

The only thing that someone in an alcoholic home is responsible for is what he does with the pain he experiences. The right response is to choose to find healing in the love and grace of God.

Work It Out: If you have an alcoholic parent
- talk to a minister about getting some help;
- find a friend who will just listen;
- become informed through, for example, your local chapter of Alcoholics Anonymous;
- work on developing your relationship with God.

He's the ultimate source of strength, comfort, and hope.

If your family isn't being shattered by alcohol, go find a friend or classmate who isn't so blessed. Listen. Help. Love. Serve. And walk with that person.

Nail It Down: Read Psalm 69. On Saturday and Sunday, work on memorizing verses 16-17. When trouble comes, pray those verses to God.

FIVE ALCOHOL

HUMAN NATURE *****
Animal, Machine, or . . . ?

The average person builds his or her theory of human nature by nailing together a wide variety of ideas—a quote from Grandma, the opinions of a favorite talk show host, and perhaps an article from *Reader's Digest*. Built on this shaky foundation of popular psychology and unproven scientific theories, the result is always a dangerous, ramshackle structure that cannot last.

Put on your hard hat and join us this week. We plan to tear down those old theories, examine the blueprint of the Master Builder, and erect a theory of human nature with the Word of God as our foundation.

"O LORD, you have searched me and you know me. . . . You are familiar with all my ways" (Psalm 139:1, 3).

Kim fell asleep before she could finish reading *The Stranger* by Albert Camus. So she got up early to finish the last chapter and review her notes for the quiz.

In the dim, early light of dawn, she thought to herself, "How depressing!"

Bingo! *The Stranger* is about a man who lives in a world of despair where God is absent and where people are alienated.

But depressing as that point of view sounds, it's commonly believed today.

Myth #1: Mankind is all alone

Look It Up: Here's something surprising: There's a Bible writer who agrees with Camus . . . to a point. In the Book of Ecclesiastes, Solomon explored life lived as if nothing existed but the physical universe. He called it living "under the sun":

"What has been will be again, what has been done will be done again; there is nothing new under the sun.

. . . I have seen all the things that are done under the sun; all of them are meaningless, a chasing after the wind" (Ecclesiastes 1: 9, 14).

The difference between Solomon and Camus is this: Solomon realized that the despairing conclusion of a universe without God showed the "universe without God" theory to be false:

"Now all has been heard; here is the conclusion of the matter: Fear God and keep his commandments, for this is the whole duty of man" (Ecclesiastes 12:13).

Think It Through: Many people throughout history have struggled with feelings of despair. After all, if God doesn't exist, we do not have a meaningful origin or a meaningful destiny. Anything goes, nothing matters, life is a cosmic mistake.

Work It Out: What's the alternative? Turn to your Creator, and find meaning and security in this world. Trust Christ, and know that you aren't alone in a strange universe. Here's a prayer for the week:

"God, I want to gain a better understanding of human nature. But more than that, I want to know You. Thank You that I am not alone in the universe. Open my eyes and change my life as I spend time in Your Word this week. Amen."

Nail It Down: Read Genesis 1.

******* ONE **HUMAN NATURE***

On this morning's talk show Kim heard a paleontologist describe his newest discovery —a bone that looks like a human rib. "This proves," the man exulted, "that a whole race of sub-human creatures roamed Africa millions of years ago. This find links us directly to our animal ancestors!"

Next up was a story about a group of animal rights activists. The leader of the group said, "We must save our fellow creatures who are being tortured in science labs around the world. All of life is valuable."

Myth # 2: Mankind is only an animal

Look It Up: The widespread idea that man is merely the highest animal in an evolutionary chain is contradicted in the opening pages of the Bible:

"So God created man in his own image, in the image of God he created him; male and female he created them. God blessed them and said to them, 'Be fruitful and increase in number; fill the earth and subdue it. Rule over the fish of the sea and the birds of the air and over every living creature that moves on the ground' " (Genesis 1:27-28).

This passage teaches that mankind was specially created by a personal God. We are not the product of chance. As rational beings who are capable of making moral choices, we are the unique reflection of God in the world.

Think It Through: Consider the horrible implications of the "man is just a complex amoeba" myth:

If our ultimate origin is valueless chance, and our ultimate destiny is equally valueless, then we are really valueless right now. Any value that people have is value in name only—it's assigned to them by other people.

If that's the case, then Hitler has an excuse. He can say that he, as the elected ruler of his nation, with support of the people, had a right to assign less value to the Jews.

And so, if you think Hitler was a murderer, you really think that humans are more than complex amoebas.

Work It Out: Read Psalm 139. Copy these verses on a sheet of paper and put it in your wallet. Every time you hear a reference to any idea that diminishes the value of humanity, pull out the sheet and read it carefully.

Nail It Down: Read Genesis 9:1-7.

Pray About It:

* * * * * * TWO

97

Kim's first hour class is Sociology with Mrs. Kaufman. Always optimistic and cheerful, Mrs. Kaufman is popular with all the students. Let's listen in.

"So you see, class, no one is born 'evil' or 'sinful.' We're simply products of our environment. Why does a ghetto kid turn to crime? Is it because he's evil? No! He doesn't have the benefits of a positive home and good education. Take that kid, educate him, and change his surroundings, and you'll lessen and possibly eliminate his negative behavior."

Myth # 3: Mankind is basically good

Look It Up: Mrs. Kaufman's lecture seems to make sense. But according to the Word of God, it simply isn't true.

We are born sinful. Or put another way, our very nature is to sin:

"You were dead in your transgressions and sins, in which you used to live when you followed the ways of this world . . . gratifying the cravings of our sinful nature and following its desires and thoughts. Like the rest, we were by nature objects of wrath" (Ephesians 2:1-3).

Think It Through: In making her claim, Mrs. Kaufman ignored some relevant evidence: For example, many criminals grew up in a great environment. If environment was all that determined behavior, wouldn't all the bad guys live in only one neighborhood?

Unfortunately, sinful human beings who need to be changed from the inside often exhibit "negative behavior" regardless of their environment.

Work It Out: The bad news is that people are sinful and separated from God. The good news is that Jesus died on the cross to solve the problem. When we trust Him to forgive us, He comes into our lives and begins to change us from the inside out. He exchanges our evil and lifelessness for His goodness and life.

Ask a friend if they think man is basically good or evil. If they respond, "good," ask why. Think about their answer. Does it take into account the terrible things people have done? Share with them the Scripture's view of human nature. Point out how it rings true considering the facts of history.

If your friend says, "evil," ask them what the solution to man's evil is. It's a great way to share your faith.

Nail It Down: Read Isaiah 53:6.

 **THREE** **HUMAN NATURE**

In psychology class, Kim and her classmates are studying about B. F. Skinner, the famous behavioral scientist.

"Skinner believed," the teacher droned, "that man is purely a 'biological system.' In other words, man doesn't have a nonphysical side. There's no soul or mind or consciousness. To him, these concepts are outdated, primitive religious beliefs. Skinner focused on the behavior of the complex machine known as man."

Everyone nodded sleepily.

Myth # 4: Mankind is purely physical

Look It Up: Scripture uses many terms to refer to the non-physical aspect of people:
1. Soul (Deuteronomy 4:29)—includes the emotional aspect.
2. Spirit. "The lamp of the LORD searches the spirit of a man; it searches out his inmost being" (Proverbs 20:27).
3. Heart (1 Timothy 1:5)—stands for the control center of one's life.
4. Conscience (Hebrews 13:18)—the inner moral voice.
5. Mind (Romans 1:28; 12:2)—perceives, understands, judges, and determines.
6. Sinful nature (Romans 7:18)—opposes God.
7. Will (1 Corinthians 7:37)—chooses.

Think It Through: Christianity is not at odds with science. In fact, since God made and ordered the universe, we can count on its regular behavior—the basis for scientific investigation.

Christianity is at odds with scientism. Scientism assumes that the natural world is all that exists. Any explanation of observed facts that appeals to a supernatural entity—for example, explaining love as something more than mere chemistry—is ruled out from the start, regardless of the evidence.

That doesn't sound very open-minded, does it?

Work It Out: If you go to a public school, and are being exposed to one-sided teaching, you have work to do:
• Ask God to protect your faith.
• Read Norman L. Geisler's *Knowing the Truth About Creation*, published by Servant Books. There is no better summary of this important issue.

Nail It Down: Read 1 Thessalonians 5:23.

Pray About It:

* * * * * * FOUR

Kim clicks the TV on and begins watching a program about the future.

The show's point is that the human race is capable of solving its own problems. At the conclusion, the narrator intones:

"We do not need ancient myths, superstition, or the baggage of religion weighing us down. Through scientific research, technology, human reason, and progressive secular education, we can not only save humanity from all of its problems, but we can also build a humane and prosperous global community."

Myth # 5: Mankind can save itself

Look It Up: Can humanity save itself? Are we really self-sufficient? According to the Bible, no and no. Mankind desperately needs the Lord.

• God alone can save. "For the LORD is our judge, the LORD is our lawgiver, the LORD is our king; it is he who will save us" (Isaiah 33:22).

• Depending on anything or anyone other than God is idolatry. " 'Ignorant are those who carry about idols of wood, who pray to gods that cannot save' " (Isaiah 45:20).

Think It Through: Our nation is facing some serious problems: drug abuse, pollution problems, crime, educational failure, the breakdown of the family, economic hardships, and Middle East madness.

All our coins bear the phrase "In God We Trust." Do you think that's true? As a nation, do you think that we look to God to deliver us?

Work It Out: You've got two assignments today.

• Ask God to bring about personal revival in your life. If you don't know Christ, trust Him right now to forgive your sins and to lead you in His ways, giving your life meaning. If you are a Christian, ask God to help you to obey Him better.

• Ask God to bring about a national revival. Only a return to Biblical truth can deliver us from the problems brought about by abandoning that truth. Pray that the Church would strengthen its witness to all areas of life—including law and government.

Nail It Down: Read Deuteronomy 13:1-11. On Saturday, read verses 12-18. On Sunday read the whole chapter again. What do you think God thinks of a nation that abandons Him?

* * * * * * * FIVE **HUMAN NATURE**

"**P**aper or plastic?" the bagboy at the grocery store asks. In your mind you think, "Who cares?"

And yet, your choice will affect the world around you. Answer paper and you indirectly vote to chop down another tree. Answer plastic and, in a roundabout way, you help drill another oil well since plastic is a petroleum product.

Small decisions—big consequences. Other choices are important as well. Driving a car instead of riding the bus contributes to the "greenhouse effect," a global warming trend caused by excessive carbon dioxide in the air. Buying aerosol hair spray or styrofoam plates means releasing chloroflourocarbons that destroy the earth's protective ozone shield. Washing clothes with detergents that contain phosphates means altering the delicate balance of life in streams, lakes and rivers.

Multiply these "little" choices by the millions of people living in overcrowded industrialized societies, throw in other pressing problems such as what to do about acid rain and nuclear waste, and it's no wonder environmentalists are concerned.

The Bible and the environment. The Bible states that after God created the heavens and the earth (Genesis 1:1), He created man and woman. Then the Creator gave His human creatures authority to "subdue" the earth (Genesis 1:28).

Some people use this command as a license for exploitation. The earth's resources are depleted in order to support extravagant and greedy lifestyles. No thought is given to the facts that these resources are limited and non-renewable or that their careless consumption contributes to the world's pollution problems.

Others see Genesis 1:28 as a call to conservation. The human race is to act as a caretaker of creation. The goal is not to conquer the environment. We are to conserve it for future use and pleasure (see Genesis 2:15).

What now? Because of the condition of our planet, Christians must be more concerned about the environment. And our concern must lead to action. Ecological preservation and protection, not pollution, should mark those who follow Christ.

Did you know that it's possible to summarize the message of each of the books of the Old Testament in three words or less? It's true. Here are the first 39 books of the Bible . . . in brief!

Old Testament Book	Its Message Summarized
Genesis	Beginnings
Exodus	Exit
Leviticus	Offerings and Feasts
Numbers	Wanders
Deuteronomy	Second Law
Joshua	Conquers
Judges	Cycles
Ruth	Love Story
1 Samuel	Saul
2 Samuel	David
1 Kings	Solomon
2 Kings	Exile
1 Chronicles	Editorial on David
2 Chronicles	Editorial on Judah
Ezra	Temple/People
Nehemiah	Walls
Esther	Queen of Persia
Job	Sovereignty
Psalms	Worship
Proverbs	Wisdom
Ecclesiastes	Emptiness
Song of Solomon	Love in Marriage
Isaiah	Groan/Glory
Jeremiah	Rotten Belt
Lamentations	Tears
Ezekiel	Dry Bones
Daniel	Dreams
Hosea	Harlot
Joel	Locusts
Amos	Plumbline
Obadiah	Brother's Keeper
Jonah	Fish
Micah	Day in Court
Nahum	Flood
Habakkuk	Watchtower
Zephaniah	Day of the Lord
Haggai	Temple
Zechariah	Messiah
Malachi	Hearts of Stone

MYTHS
Exposing False Notions

"The discerning heart seeks knowledge, but the mouth of a fool feeds on folly" (Proverbs 15:14).

A myth is like a birthday package without a gift. Though nicely wrapped on the outside, it turns out to be empty on the inside.

But if you think myths ended with ancient Rome, I'd like you to meet the Brightsides, a nice Christian family. Each Brightside believes a different modern myth.

Let's spend a week with this family. Who knows? You might discover that you believe some empty myths too!

B ill Brightside makes a few calls on his carphone as he waits in traffic. "Time is money, right?" he asks rhetorically as he wheels and deals with clients. We finally arrive at his corporate headquarters. He leads the way into a spacious and very elegant office. We sit down.

"My business philosophy is simple," he begins. "I grew up poor and I know that without money, you just can't do much in this world, right?

"Now, I admit, my 14-hour days keep me away from the family and church. But I like to think of all this as making money for God."

Trusting in material wealth

Look It Up: Okay, Mr. Brightside, are you making money for God? Or are you making money your god? A lot of people buy into the idea that money means happiness. But it's not necessarily so.

Jesus told the story of a foolish rich man who said to himself, " 'You have plenty of good things laid up for many years. Take life easy; eat, drink and be merry.'

"But God said to him, 'You fool! This very night your life will be demanded from you. Then who will get what you have prepared for yourself?'

"This is how it will be with anyone who stores up things for himself but is not rich toward God" (Luke 12:19–21).

Think It Through: Money can be stolen, jewelry can be lost, property can be seized or destroyed. There's never a time when any of it is guaranteed 100 percent safe! The view that money is ultimately trustworthy is a modern myth.

Do you know Christians like Mr. Brightside? Are you like him?

Work It Out: If you answered yes to that last question, do two things:

• Pray. "Father, I have an idol. I trust more in material things than I do in You. I know that's wrong. Please change me. Show me ways to decrease my dependence on things. Cause my trust in You to increase—by the power of Christ. Amen."

• Reflect on 1 Timothy 6:17–19 every day this week.

Then, if you have extra material possessions or wealth, willingly use some to help someone less fortunate. (See Acts 4:32-35.)

Nail It Down: Read Proverbs 11:28.

ONE MYTHS

Today Bonnie Brightside, 17, is feeling pretty grown-up and very ready to get out from under the thumb of her over-protective mother. She wants to hurry up and get to college and experience life on her own.

Sitting in her bedroom, Bonnie opens up. "All Mom lets me do is go to church. I miss out on all the fun in life! I'm dying to know whats it's like to be the life of the party . . . to get high and really loosen up . . . to make love to a handsome stranger. Well, my life may be boring right now, but when I get to college I'm really going to make up for lost time."

Thinking that sin brings fulfillment

Look It Up: Bonnie is on the verge of making some big mistakes. She believes the myth that sin satisfies. But that's been the devil's lie since the beginning of time.

" 'You will not surely die,' the serpent said to the woman. 'For God knows that when you eat of it your eyes will be opened, and you will be like God, knowing good and evil.'

"When the woman saw that the fruit of the tree was good for food and pleasing to the eye, and also desirable for gaining wisdom, she took some and ate it. She also gave some to her husband" (Genesis 3:4-6).

The result? Sorrow, tragedy, death. In a word, sin brought dissatisfaction, both divine and human. ●

Think It Through: The rich, exotic dishes look too good to pass up. So you eat. The food tastes too good to believe. But then you realize the chef is really a deranged murderer. You've been poisoned!

Satan does that. He always makes sin look appealing and enticing. But those who eat end up burned.

Work It Out: Here are 3 R's for avoiding this world's favorite myth—the idea that sin satisfies:

• Renew your mind. Change your way of thinking! Cut out the worldly input—the movies, TV, magazines, songs—that make light of sin and warp your values.

• Recognize temptations when they come. Be on your guard. Otherwise, you could be fooled by some innocent-looking bait.

• Reject the offer to sin. Think about the consequences, especially about displeasing the Lord, who loved you enough to die for you.

Nail It Down: Read Hebrews 11:24-28.

Pray About It: ───────────

◆◆◆◆◆◆◆

T W O

Mrs. Betty Brightside is a very pretty woman who attends an aerobics class faithfully. Always well-dressed, she makes sure that her home is spotless. She's proud of her public image and of the status she and her husband have in the community.

"I think people ought to be able to look at us Christians and see a difference," she says. "For example, take that Jo Ellen Nash who works at the church. She's the sweetest thing, helping like she does with the homeless. But the poor thing needs to lose at least 75 pounds! Her appearance is just awful!"

Overemphasizing external things

Look It Up: Mrs. Brightside is right. Christians should be different. However, the difference must be more than merely external. Jesus said people can look great on the outside and still be rotten on the inside.

" 'Woe to you, teachers of the law and Pharisees, you hypocrites! You are like whitewashed tombs, which look beautiful on the outside but on the inside are full of dead men's bones and everything unclean' " (Matthew 23:27).

He also said, "Stop judging by mere appearances, and make a right judgment" (John 7:24).

Think It Through: Is it wrong to look nice or try to get in shape or to have nice clothes? No! But it is wrong to have a "Betty Brightside" perspective on life and judge everyone and everything by outer appearance.

Did the rag-tag band of disciples who followed Jesus have a good public image? Not if "good public image" means they possessed the symbols of success.

How do you think God views success and spirituality? Can a person have only one or the other? Can a person have both?

Work It Out: Say no to the myth that external appearance is more important than internal health. Here's how:

• Don't isolate the spiritual from the physical. View all the events of life—personal grooming, exercise, school, work, prayer, Bible reading—as God's gifts to you for the advancement of His kingdom.

• Quit judging other people on the basis of appearance. Don't write people off just because they are short, overweight, handicapped, poor, or different from you in some other way.

Nail It Down: Read 2 Corinthians 10:7.

THREE MYTHS

Nice-looking, smart, a good athlete, popular—that's Biff Brightside.

People are always telling him how talented he is. And it's true. He doesn't really have to work to make good grades, friends, or touchdowns.

Biff thinks he's got the world by the tail.

"I feel really confident in my abilities. If I put my mind to something, I know I can do it. Things have always come pretty easy for me so far, but even if I get in a tough situation, I don't have any doubt that I can handle it. I know I can come out on top through hard work."

Trusting only in yourself

Look It Up: What many people consider the admirable quality of confidence is often nothing more than cockiness—trusting only in one's own abilities. To such an attitude, God's Word says:

• " 'Cursed is the one who trusts in man, who depends on flesh for his strength and whose heart turns away from the LORD' " (Jeremiah 17:5).

• "He who trusts in himself is a fool, but he who walks in wisdom is kept safe" (Proverbs 28:26).

• "So, if you think you are standing firm, be careful that you don't fall!" (1 Corinthians 10:12).

Sheesh. So much for self-sufficiency.

Think It Through: Do you count on solely your own ability to ace that English exam; make that free throw; land a date for the weekend; talk to someone about the Lord; put together a project; impress your employer; make new friends; or talk in front of a group? If so, you've got a pride problem.

Work It Out: Here are some tips for abandoning the myth of self-sufficiency:

1. Confess. Thoughts like "I can do this on my own" or "Look at what I've done without any help from anyone!" are offensive to God (Daniel 4:30-32).

2. Submit. Jesus Christ is Lord. Lord means master. Because of who He is, you must do what He wants and depend ultimately on His strength (Psalm 28:7).

3. Pray. Ask God to sanctify every activity in which you're involved (1 Thessalonians 5:17). It's hard to trust in yourself while you're talking to God.

Nail It Down: Read Isaiah 2:22.

Pray About It:

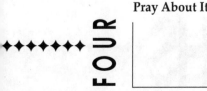

FOUR

✦✦✦✦✦✦✦

B ob Brightside is Bonnie's twin brother. He's also eager to get that high school diploma because he's already got his whole life planned out.

"I'm going to go to the University of Virginia and study finance and international relations. Then I'm going to get a law degree and start my own import–exporting firm with offices all over the world."

What about church responsibilities and a close walk with Christ?

"I'll worry about all that when I'm older, married, and ready to settle down and have a family."

Presuming on the future

Look It Up: One of the great modern myths is assuming that we have the right and ability to dictate our own future. James offers a different perspective:

"Now listen, you who say, 'Today or tomorrow we will go to this or that city, spend a year there, carry on business and make money.' Why, you do not even know what will happen tomorrow. What is your life? You are a mist that appears for a little while and then vanishes. Instead, you ought to say, 'If it is the Lord's will, we will live and do this or that.' As it is you boast and brag. All such boasting is evil" (James 4:13–16).

Think It Through: Is it wrong to make plans for the future? Is it wrong to live as though we alone were the masters of our destiny? Remember: God is the Lord of history; nobody escapes from His gaze; and no plans we make fool Him or overrule Him.

Work It Out: Don't plan your life independently. Plan your world in light of God's Word. For example, here are some pointers in planning a career:

1. Look at the way God has made you. What are you good at? What do you enjoy? What are your strengths? Your weaknesses?

2. Look for a career that fits the way God made you. Is there a field that interests you? Given your strengths, would you be good at it?

3. Pray. Ask God to move history in your life to confirm or deny the direction you want to go. And ask Him to prevent you from making anything—including a career—an idol.

Nail It Down: Read Proverbs 19:21. On Saturday, read Proverbs 16:9. On Sunday, read Proverbs 16:3 for a real encouragement.

FIVE MYTHS

REJECTION

Getting Past the Pain

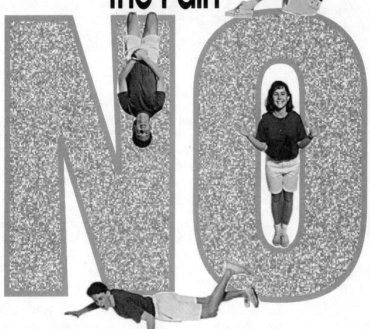

Rejection comes in   many packages. A dating relationship
ends. A home is shattered by separation or divorce. Friends mis-
treat or ignore one of their own. The bad news is that for many people
rejection is a painful fact of life.

Would you like to hear the good news? The Bible has real answers for
those who struggle with feelings of rejection.

Discover this week the wonder of God's great love and acceptance!

"In all these things we are more than conquerors through him who loved us"
(Romans 8:37).

B rian is not having a good day.

He's new at Adams High School. No one sits by him at lunch. During P. E. class, nobody picks him to participate. In fact, three bigger guys pick on him in front of some girls. Brian feels humiliated.

Patti is in tears. She just found out that her two closest friends are having a party. They've invited everybody–except her. When she walks to her locker after school, her two "friends" giggle as she passes by.

A large order of acceptance to go

Look It Up: Brian and Patti are going through tough situations. But they're not alone. Every person that ever lived has experienced similar circumstances.

And while it's true that we can't control how others treat us, we can control one thing—how we react.

When you're feeling hurt, these truths can make a big difference:

• Because God created you in His image, He considers you precious and valuable (Genesis 1:26; Psalm 139:13-16).

• God loves you more than you can comprehend (Romans 5:8).

• God is there to care for you even when it seems nobody else is (Matthew 10:29-31)

• God is "the Father of compassion and the God of all comfort, who comforts us in all our troubles, so that we can comfort those in any trouble with the comfort we ourselves have received from God" (2 Corinthians 1:3-4).

Think It Through: Regardless of how rejected you may feel, regardless of how unkind others have been, you can know without a doubt that God feels differently about you than those who have rejected you. He'll never be cruel to you or cast you aside. He created you and He's a friend you can depend on.

Work It Out: If you're feeling like Brian or Patti for some reason, take a few moments right now to open yourself up to God. Tell Him just how you feel.

But don't stop there; Let Him tell you about how much you matter to Him. Look up the verses above and think about them. Be willing to share what you find with others who feel the bitter pain of rejection.

Nail It Down: Read Isaiah 43:1-7.

xxxxxxxxx ONE REJECTION xxx

Getting to the heart of the matter

I can't believe this," thought Jennifer to herself. "Holly, the weirdest girl at school, is sitting at my lunch table. Will you look at her outfit? Does she wash? She's rambling to me like we're best friends or something. I'm so embarrassed."

Holly's voice trailed off to a whisper. "I know you need to study. But I sat down because I don't know where else to turn. I know you're a Christian, and I've been wondering a lot lately about God and stuff. Can you help me?"

Look It Up: Jennifer swallowed hard as she remembered what she had read that morning in her Bible. "The LORD does not look at the things man looks at. Man looks at the outward appearance, but the LORD looks at the heart" (1 Samuel 16:7).

She had always blown Holly off because of her outward appearance. She would never have guessed that Holly was hungry to know more about God.

A few weeks later, Jennifer said to another friend, "I had Holly figured all wrong. She's different for sure, but really sweet and a lot of fun when you get to know her. And I'm really glad I can be a witness to her."

When God looks at people, He doesn't see their clothes, their makeup, hairstyles, or reputation. God sees each person's heart. He gets past the superficial stuff to discover what an individual is really about.

Think It Through: Which matters more to you, outer credentials or inner potential?

Looking at others from God's perspective demands that we not reject them for the way they seem on the outside. We must try to get to know them on the inside.

We are responsible to discover the potential in others and encourage them to achieve their best in God's kingdom. Think about it: What a privilege it is to be able to share God's unconditional love with those who have felt the sting of rejection.

Work It Out: Right now think of someone you know who gets rejected because he or she is different. Ask God to grant you the insight to see as He sees— not just external characteristics, but internal character. Then determine to go out of your way to encourage that person.

Nail It Down: Meditate on 1 Chronicles 28:9.

Pray About It: _____

X X X X X X   TWO

111

Two hours ago, Jim was having a great time at a friend's house. But when the NC-17 movie went into the VCR, Jim went home.

Jim said to his Mom: "Man, Mom, it sure hurts. The guys looked at me like I was some kind of freak when I told them I wouldn't feel right seeing that movie."

"Just remember, son, that your non-Christian friends may ridicule you when you follow Christ. Why don't you see if a couple of your friends from church would like to come over. I'll order a pizza and you can watch the game on television."

"Thanks, Mom."

Feeling good abou feeling bad

Look It Up: "If you suffer as a Christian, do not be ashamed, but praise God that you bear that name" (1 Peter 4:16).

As Christians, we are sometimes limited in our relationships with non-Christians. They don't see the world the same way we do; they have a different worldview.

Like Jim, then, we'll sometimes have to make decisions that are unpopular with our friends. As a result, we may feel rejected by those who either can't understand why or don't like the fact that our commitment to Christ comes first.

Many times, though, these feelings of rejection are only in our own minds. Our non-Christian friends often actually respect—rather than reject—us for having the courage to stand up for what we believe.

But even when the rejection is real, we can find comfort in God's nearness (Psalm 34:18) and in His promise to reward our faithfulness to Him (Matthew 5:10-12).

Think It Through: Do you ever fear you will be rejected if you refuse to go along with some of your non-Christian friends' behavior? Do you think if you had been in Jim's shoes you would have done what he did?

It's important to have relationships with unbelievers so that we can be witnesses for Christ. But it's also crucial that we not compromise our convictions just to avoid catching grief from our friends.

Work It Out: Try to envision a typical day at school and the different opportunities for either courage or compromise that commonly arise.

Pray for the courage to stand up for what you believe. Then commit your fear of rejection to God.

Nail It Down: Memorize Psalm 1:1-3.

xxxxxxxxx THREE REJECTION xx>

112

Jill is devastated. Her boyfriend, Mike, told her that he thought it would be best for them to date around. Almost immediately he began going out with Missy.

Jill feels rejected and depressed. She imagines God is punishing her for something. She also would like to get even with Mike.

Susan just got "dumped" too. She was really crazy about Randy, but suddenly he quit calling—no explanations, no big breakup scene, nothing! Susan tried to talk to him several times, but he wouldn't give her any reasons.

Recovery from romantic rejection

Look It Up: Susan is understandably sad and confused. But she seems to be handling the break-up a lot better than Jill. She doesn't seem to be bitter at God or Randy. She isn't acting like her life is over. And she's actually enjoying dating some other guys.

Here's some good advice: Be like Susan. When a dating relationship ends, remember that

• God is sovereign over all your circumstances, and He is wise in bringing those circumstances to pass: "Will not the Judge of all the earth do right?" (Genesis 18:25);

• God feels for you: "The LORD is gracious and compassionate, . . . good to all; he has compassion on all he has made" (Psalm 145:8-9).

Think It Through: The reason Susan was better able to handle her traumatic breakup is because she took refuge in the Lord. That doesn't mean her breakup wasn't painful. But Susan was able to keep her break-up with Randy in proper perspective by reflecting on Biblical truths and then putting them into practice—even when she didn't really feel like it.

Work It Out: Are you suffering from romantic rejection? Try this prescription:
• Be honest with God about your true feelings.
• Trust God's goodness in the hard times (Psalm 27:13-14).
• Refuse to allow bitterness to spring up in your heart (Colossians 3:12-15).

Take the Master's medicine and see just how much you'll improve. If you have a good friend who's lovesick, share the antidote with him or her.

Nail It Down: Read Psalm 30.

Pray About It:

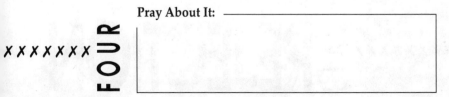

X X X X X X X FOUR

Greg just can't stop thinking about Bill. Last week Bill told him that his parents were thinking about getting a divorce. Today he listened in shock as Bill, who was crying, described his parents' most recent argument:

"I'm sick of all of you. That's why I'm leaving!"

"Fine! Go ahead! But you're not gonna stick me with these kids. I can't control them and you know it!"

"Oh, yeah? Well, if you don't get the kids, you don't get the house!"

Greg didn't know what to say. What in the world can he say or do to help his hurting friend?

When rejection comes home

Look It Up: The next morning as Greg is reading his Bible, he comes across a verse that intrigues him: "All that the Father gives me will come to me, and whoever comes to me I will never drive away" (John 6:37).

"Wow," Greg thinks. "Those who turn to Christ will find complete acceptance in Christ. Hey, that's a verse I need to share with Bill."

Think It Through: Greg realizes he can't make Bill's parents act differently. Nor can he really understand what it must be like to live in a home full of conflict, feeling like nobody cares.

But Greg decides to do what he can. He can be a great friend to Bill, providing support and comfort through the rough times. He can share with Bill the love and acceptance that God has for him. And he can pray regularly and fervently for God to work a miracle in Bill's family. In short, Greg can do a lot to minimize Bill's horrible feelings of rejection.

Work It Out: Can you relate to what Greg or Bill are facing? Chances are at least one of your friends is going through tough times at home, perhaps feeling rejected and unloved. Ask God to give you the sensitivity to know when your friends are hurting and the wisdom to know what to say.

If you find yourself in Bill's situation, find comfort in the love and acceptance Christ offers. And find a good friend like Greg who'll be there when you need him.

Nail It Down: Read Psalm 37:5-7. On Saturday and Sunday, read about the most horrible rejection of all time: God's rejection of Christ in our place (Matthew 27).

x x x x x x x x x FIVE REJECTION x x x

FRIENDSHIP
How Do You Measure Up?

"*Greater love has no one than this, that he lay down*
s life for his friends" (John 15:13).

Perhaps you've seen wrinkled old men sitting on a park bench and watched them love and laugh, endure and enjoy one another, counsel and comfort each other. Is it a mystery? Or is it a miracle?

Friendship.

It's that amazing commitment that means you don't have to put up a front. You can be yourself. You're safe, liked, accepted.

Friendship.

It's more valuable than anything this world has to offer— and more costly. It involves more than doling out a few bucks. You have to give yourself. But you get back more than you ever dreamed.

The Wagners moved to Denver almost eight months ago.

Karen, 14, has yet to make a friend. She sits around watching television and listening to music. She's bored out of her mind.

Sixteen-year-old Helen, on the other hand, has made friends with almost everybody in town. She's always doing stuff, going to parties, and getting asked out. Problem is, she's hanging out with a crowd that is definitely on the wild side. It's to the point that she's seriously hurting her walk with God.

Which of the Wagner girls is in worse shape?

Use your head to choose friends

Look It Up: Friendship is more than just finding a group to run around with. In fact, by picking your pals too quickly and without much thought, it's possible to end up with "friends" who really aren't friends after all. This is why the Bible warns us to choose our friends wisely:

"A righteous man is cautious in friendship, but the way of the wicked leads them astray" (Proverbs 12:26).

Another verse points out that "a man of many companions may come to ruin, but there is a friend who sticks closer than a brother" (Proverbs 18:24).

Finally, we are urged to watch out for people who just want to use us (Proverbs 19:6-7).

Think It Through: Think about your circle of friends. How many of those people genuinely care about you? How many of them would stick closer to you than a brother during a crisis? Are any of them using you because of your popularity, money, looks, or abilities?

Work It Out: Let's face it. Christians should have relationships with people who don't know Christ. How else can we be witnesses for Him? The problem comes when we let those friendships pull us away from the truth.

If you're involved in a close friendship that's hurting your walk with God, rearrange your priorities. Don't completely walk away from the friendship, but be more cautious. If you're trying to be the best friend to everyone in your whole school, stop and evaluate. Two or three quality friendships are much more valuable than knowing the names of a thousand people.

Here's a prayer for the week: "Lord, I want to learn how the be the best friend I can be. Change me this week as I study what your Word says. Amen."

Nail It Down: Read Deuteronomy 13:6-10.

• • • • • • • • • • ONE **FRIENDSHIP** • • •

Wise lips build strong friendships

Vance and Mark have been best friends as long as they can remember. As kids they played little league sports together and were in the same Cub Scout Troop. Now they go to the same church and school.

But lately they've drifted apart. Vance feels weird because Mark has started drinking with some rowdy guys on weekends.

And Mark is mad because Vance told some girls at church what is going on.

Sounds like a case of broken-down communication.

Look It Up: Good friendships mean that we must communicate with our friends truthfully.

We need to *confront* our friends when they get out of hand: "Better is open rebuke than hidden love. Wounds from a friend can be trusted, but an enemy multiplies kisses" (Proverbs 27:5-6).

In other words, sometimes the truth hurts.

We need to *counsel* our friends when they need direction: "Perfume and incense bring joy to the heart, and the pleasantness of one's friend springs from his earnest counsel" (Proverbs 27:9).

Think It Through: Let's play the "Stupid/Smart" game! You decide whether a response is stupid or smart.

• Because of a big fight with her parents, 14-year-old Beth decides to run away. Her best friend Tricia knows Beth is overreacting and is making a big mistake, but she doesn't tell her what she thinks.

• At 6 feet 4 inches, Carl would love to try out for the basketball team. But he's not too confident. He asks his friend Randy what to do, and Randy replies, "How should I know? Do I look like a jock?"

Work It Out: Maybe God wants you to confront your straying friends about an attitude or action that needs changing. Ask for wisdom to say the right things. Be careful not to come across with a "I'm-holier-than-you-attitude." If they act mad or hurt at first, that's normal. They'll get over it—if they're really true friends.

You may need to counsel close friends who need direction. Listen carefully and offer solid advice that squares with the wisdom of the Word.

Speaking the truth in love makes strong friendships.

Nail It Down: Read Proverbs 28:23.

Pray About It:

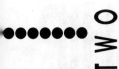

TWO

Craig is a new Christian who has only been coming to church for a short time. Yesterday he pulled one of the youth leaders aside and said, "I don't know how to say this, but sometimes this place gives me the creeps."

"What do you mean? Why?"

"Well, the girls are always hugging each other every 15 minutes and saying, 'I love you' to their friends. And some of the men go up and hug each other! If you ask me it looks gay."

Friendship starts in the heart

Look It Up: One of the best examples of friendship in Scripture is the close relationship between Jonathan and David.

How unlikely! Two brave, battle-hardened warriors. Men of strength and courage . . . and yet, not ashamed to show their love for each other.

In time, a jealous King Saul determined to kill David. In an emotional farewell, Jonathan told his best friend to flee: "Then they kissed each other and wept together —but David wept the most. Jonathan said to David, 'Go in peace, for we have sworn friendship with each other in the name of the Lord' " (1 Samuel 20:41-42).

Think It Through: Our culture says "macho" guys shouldn't express emotion. What a warped idea! Expressions of affection don't mean you're strange. They're completely normal! Jonathan and David were two incredibly "macho" men (in a culture where kissing is like our shaking hands) who never gave a second thought to expressing how they felt about one other.

Why can most girls tell each other "I love you" without batting an eyelash? Why can't guys? How come girls are not afraid to get emotional and share their feelings with each other? Why don't guys usually do that?

Work It Out: Perhaps right now you can't see yourself saying to your friend, "Hey, I really love and appreciate you." That's okay. At least you can start doing more to show how much you care.

And meanwhile, sit down with some friends and discuss this idea of expressing emotion. Using Jonathan and David as an example, try to figure out why verbal expressions of love are hard for so many people.

Nail It Down: Read 1 Samuel 18:1-3.

•••••••••• THREE **FRIENDSHIP** •••

Everybody knows Jason. He's one of the biggest (and best) players on the football team. He's hilarious. All the members of the "in" crowd at school love to be around him.

Drew is a different story. He's not very athletic or funny or "cool." It's not that people dislike him. They just ignore him. Everyone, that is, except Jason. You can believe it or not, but Jason and Drew are best friends. They go hunting and fishing together all the time and always have a blast.

It takes guts and an iron will

Look It Up: Drew and Jason became friends when they were kids, and they've stayed close even while pursuing different interests. How? Because they understand that true friendship requires that we commit to our friends unconditionally. Consider these wise sayings:

"A friend loves at all times, and a brother is born for adversity" (Proverbs 17:17).

"Do not forsake your friend and the friend of your father, and do not go to your brother's house when disaster strikes you—better a neighbor nearby than a brother far away" (Proverbs 27:10).

Both of these verses stress the importance of commitment in friendship . . . no matter what happens.

Think It Through: Commitment means you stick up for a friend when everyone else is trashing him or her. It means you keep in touch. It means you can be counted on when trouble is brewing. It means you don't let minor differences diminish your relationship.

Work It Out: Take these steps to become a more committed friend:

• Pray for your friends today and everyday.

• Approach a friend with whom you've had a strained relationship lately. Talk about and resolve whatever problem is hampering your friendship.

• Find a friend who is in trouble and who needs someone to believe in him or her. This doesn't mean that you condone the wrong actions, only that you stand with your friend and continue loving no matter what.

• Comfort a friend who is going through a difficult experience. It might not be convenient to go out of your way to help, but that's what commitment requires.

Nail It Down: Read Proverbs 27:17.

Pray About It:

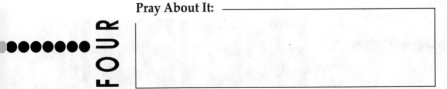

FOUR

119

Early on a rainy Monday morning the dreaded phone call finally came. Walt's dad, after a long struggle with lung cancer, died.

While the family huddled together at the hospital, their friends swung into action. People from church brought food, cleaned house, and volunteered to house out-of-town funeral guests. Walt's two best friends left school to come by and sit with their dazed friend. They didn't say much, but just being there was a huge support.

The hands and fee of friendship

Look It Up: Walt's family was blessed by people who understood the Biblical principle that true friendship involves sacrifice.

• "Two are better than one, because they have a good return for their work: If one falls down, his friend can help him up. But pity the man who falls and has no one to help him up! . . . Though one may be overpowered, two can defend themselves. A cord of three strands is not quickly broken" (Ecclesiastes 4:9-12).

• "Julius, in kindness to Paul, allowed him to go to his friends so they might provide for his needs" (Acts 27:3).

Think It Through: This week we've seen the importance of choosing friends wisely with your head, communicating truthfully with your mouth, caring deeply with your heart, committing unconditionally with your will, and, finally today, contributing sacrificially with your hands and feet.

Can your chosen friends count on you for communication, caring, commitment, and sacrifice?

Work It Out: Use your hands and feet today to develop deeper friendships. This means action. It means being willing to sacrifice your time, emotion, energy, and even material wealth if necessary for your friends.

Today, use your hands to support friends with pats on the back, hugs, and assistance in doing tasks. Also today, use your feet to walk with friends in times of hurt and to go to whatever lengths are necessary to meet their needs. Go out of your way to help them.

Nail It Down: Read 1 Samuel 18:4. On Saturday, read about Christ's model friendship and the way we are to show Him our friendship—John 15:13-14. On Sunday, memorize Saturday's passage.

•••••••••• FIVE FRIENDSHIP ••

SUMMERTIME
A N D   T H E   B I B L E

• Did you know the beach is a great picture of how much God loves you? Next time you go, try counting the grains of sand there. Then realize this fact: God's thoughts of you outnumber all the grains of sand in the world! (See Psalm 139:17-18.)

• School is only mentioned once in the Bible (Acts 19:9), which is probably more times than you mention it during the summer.

• Abraham was apparently an advocate of summertime camping. Genesis 18:1 says, "He was sitting at the entrance to his tent in the heat of the day."

• Jesus and His disciples provided the eats at several Jewish picnics. (See Mark 6:30-44 and Mark 8:1-9.)

• Simon Peter once stayed with a friend known as Simon the tanner. They called him this, not—contrary to popular belief—because he had a darker tan than Peter, but because he tanned hides and skins for a living. (See Acts 10:6.)

• One of the Apostle Paul's favorite hangouts was the beach. (See Acts 21:5 and 27:40.)

• Peter was probably a great swimmer—maybe even an expert body surfer. (See John 21:7.)

• Once God stopped the sun in the middle of the sky for almost a whole day in order to help his people win a battle. (We're talking 24 straight peak tanning hours! See Joshua 10:12-14.)

• Ecclesiastes is a great book to read at the beach. The phrase "under the sun" is found in it 29 times!

• In God's kingdom "the moon will shine like the sun" (Moonburn, anyone? See Isaiah 30:26.)

• Hezekiah was in the pool-building business. (See 2 Kings 20:20.)

• Jesus healed a crippled man who was lying next to a pool. (See John 5:1-9.)

STATEMENTS
YOU WON'T FIND IN THE BIBLE

"Cleanliness is next to godliness."
The statement is reputed to have come from the ancient writings of the Hebrew rabbis. John Wesley, the founder of the Methodist Church, is also known to have said this.

"The Devil made me do it."
This is commonly heard when people do something naughty. Though Satan does tempt us and does try to destroy us, he has no power to make us do anything. We can only point the finger at ourselves.

"I am god. You are god. We are all god."
"If you wish to find god, look within yourself, for he is part of all of us."
Statements like these are becoming more common as New Age thought (that is, Eastern mysticism) becomes more and more popular in this country. The high priestess of the movement, Shirley MacLaine, is doing her best to promote this totally unscriptural idea that "God is all, and within all."

God is not all. He is omnipresent yet distinct from His creation.

God is not within all. He dwells in His children (John 1:12). Unlike the life-force god of the New Agers, the one true God is personal and knowable.

"Money is the root of all evil."
What the Bible really say is that "the love of money is a root of all kinds of evil" (1 Timothy 6:10).

"There is no right or wrong—just what works for you."
"Go with the flow."
"If it feels good, do it."
"There are no absolutes—everything is relative."
All of these slogans, part of the "bumpersticker philosophy" in this country, may be attributed to a secular mindset that resists authority and values personal freedom and the pursuit of pleasure. You won't find any of these in the Bible.

PROBLEMS
Everybody's Got 'Em!

I t's always something. Your car gets a flat tire in the rain. You lose your English notebook. Your toast (buttered and jellied) lands face down in your lap. You study the wrong chapter for the test. A "friend" stabs you in the back.

Will the trials of life affect you? Of course. The question isn't whether trials will affect you, but how you will respond when they do.

The next five pages are dedicated to everyone. Because everyone "wrassles" with hassles.

"Blessed is the man who perseveres under trial, because when he has stood the test, he will receive the crown of life that God has promised to those who love him" (James 1:12).

It's been a wild week for the Wood twins.

On Tuesday Sherri wrapped her mom's Oldsmobile around a telephone pole. And now her right leg is wrapped in a cast!

On the day before graduation Sheila developed a severe case of chicken pox. Looking at herself in the bathroom mirror, Sheila laments, "This is the all-time worst! Couldn't God at least have waited another couple of days?"

In the bedroom Sherri stares at the big hunk of plaster that encases her broken leg and says, "No kidding. If He treats His friends like this, it's no wonder He has so many enemies."

Hang on, . . . here comes trouble

Look It Up: Rough times are a fact of life—and Christians aren't exempt. "Consider it pure joy, my brothers, whenever you face trials of many kinds" (James 1:2).

"In this [God's salvation] you greatly rejoice, though now for a little while you may have had to suffer grief in all kinds of trials" (1 Peter 1:6).

Isn't it interesting that neither James nor Peter seemed shocked at the notion that Christians can expect to face trials? James considered them a certainty, saying we should rejoice when, not if, they come. And Peter recognized the wide variety of problems in this world, saying that life contains "all kinds of" hassles.

Think It Through: Have you ever heard a Christian say that it's never God's will for one of His followers to suffer or go through hard times?

If that's true, what do we say about all the godly people in the Bible who suffered through some really difficult situations—people like Job, the Old Testament prophets, and the early church, including the Apostle Paul?

Work It Out: Hard times are inevitable. And not only are trials guaranteed to come your way (even if your relationship with God is great), they'll also come in all shapes and sizes. But you don't have to be blown away. You can learn this week how to handle the hassles of life.

Begin by praying this prayer: "God, my life is full of problems. Sometimes I look at all the things going wrong in my life and wonder, 'What's the use?' Please show me how to use all these bad circumstances to get closer to You. Open my eyes and my heart as I read these next few pages, for the sake of Your Son. Amen."

Nail It Down: Read Proverbs 2:1-5.

ONE PROBLEMS

124

Cedric is his school's star pitcher. But he'll miss the state play-offs this week because of bad grades. He says, "Why did God let this happen?"

Denise has had one date in all of high school. And that was over two years ago. "Guys just don't call me," she complains. "Why?"

Clay feels frustrated and angry. Despite carefully following the dermatologist's instructions, his skin is still a mess. "This is just great!" he yells. "How am I supposed to go to school when my face looks like a close-up of the moon? Why do zits even exist anyway?"

The point behind the pain

Look It Up: The Bible gives several reasons for all the problems in our lives.

• Problems bring about maturity—"The testing of your faith develops perseverance. Perseverance must finish its work so that you may be mature and complete, not lacking anything" (James 1:3-4).

• Problems build character—"We know that suffering produces perseverance; perseverance, character; and character, hope" (Romans 5:3-4).

• Problems show that our faith is real—"These [trials] have come so that your faith . . . may be proved genuine and may result in praise, glory and honor when Jesus Christ is revealed" (1 Peter 1:7).

Think It Through: How often does a kid learn to ride a bike without skinning at least one knee? The point? In order to mature, we have to accept the bumps and bruises of life.

Do you know how diamonds are produced? A hunk of carbon is subjected to tremendous heat and incredible pressure for a long, long, time. The result is a dazzling diamond (much more precious than carbon!).

Work It Out: Are you ticked off at God for allowing bad circumstances in your life? Are you wondering "Why?" How about praying this prayer?

"Father, I'm facing _____ (name the trials you're dealing with) and I feel _____ (describe your emotions). Help me work with You and not fight against You. I don't feel thankful for these things but, by faith I am thanking You for being in control and for promising to work all this out for good. Amen."

Nail It Down: Read 1 Thessalonians 5:18.

Pray About It: ───────────────────────────

T W O

▼▼▼▼▼▼▼

125

As soon as he walks into the locker room, the jokes start:

"Did you guys hear about Tony? He went on some church retreat last weekend and got all religious."

"No way! Tony? Tony Minelli?"

"That's right. You got 'born again,' didn't you, Tony?" (Laughter throughout the locker room)

(Sarcastically:) "Tell us about it, Tony! Tell us about you and Jesus!"

"Yeah, preach us a little sermon!"

(Loud laughter)

When the problem is persecution

Look It Up: Maybe a scene like that never happens at your school. Then again, maybe it does.

But regardless of the tolerance for Christians at your school, make no mistake about it: when Christians stand up for what they believe, they can expect to undergo some persecution.

"Remember the words I spoke to you: 'No servant is greater than his master.' If they persecuted me, they will persecute you also" (John 15:20).

"In fact, everyone who wants to live a godly life in Christ Jesus will be persecuted" (2 Timothy 3:12).

Think It Through: Are you getting persecuted for your Christian beliefs? If not, how do you reconcile your persecution-free life with the promises above?

Persecution might be harsh, physical abuse. It might take the form of emotional abuse (friends turning their backs on you). Or it might consist of verbal abuse (jokes, putdowns and rude remarks). But no matter how you slice it, persecution is a painful problem.

Work It Out: If you're not undergoing any criticism for your beliefs, it doesn't mean that you ought to go out and ask someone, "Would you please persecute me?" But it is a good sign that maybe you ought to examine your life to see if you're really living for the Lord.

If you are catching flak because of your stand for Christ, respond as Peter did. First, maintain your commitment to God (Acts 5:29; 1 Peter 4:19). Second, rejoice that you even get to know Christ and represent Him, and that His Spirit is with you in the midst of persecution (1 Peter 4:12-16). Third, continue to do what is right and good (Acts 5:42; 1 Peter 4:19).

Nail It Down: Read 1 Corinthians 4:12.

THREE **PROBLEMS**

126

R ight before
exam week,
Tammy's parents
split up. Under-
standably, she
freaked out. She
couldn't concen-
trate on anything
and walked
around in a daze
for about two
weeks. Just long
enough to really
blow her average.

Now, four
months later, not
only is her family
falling apart, but
her dream of
a scholarship is
about to go "poof."

Yet, in spite of
everything, Tammy
has a great attitude.
She keeps saying, "I
just have to keep
believing that God
is in control.
Somehow He's
going to work all
this mess out for
good."

Try to keep track of what's true

Look It Up: Remember the story of Joseph? Betrayed
by his own brothers and sold as a slave, he ended up in
Egypt where he was wrongly accused of rape and put
in prison! There he remained—for two full years—
before he was finally released. But once out of prison,
Joseph became the Pharoah's right-hand man.

In the meantime a severe famine forced Joseph's
brothers to come to him to ask for grain. As you read
the story, you think "Now he's finally gonna get to pay
them back. This'll be good!"

But instead of taking revenge, Joseph said, "You
intended to harm me, but God intended it for good to
accomplish what is now being done, the saving of
many lives" (Genesis 50:20).

Think It Through: How would you have responded if
you had been Joseph? Or Tammy? When things start
getting crazy, why is it so important to remember that
God is in control of your situation?

Remember: If God is in control, then not only does He
know what's going on, but He's also able to accomplish
something good—even in a bad situation (Romans 8:28).

Work It Out: Pick out the biggest trial you face. Now
for a few minutes, try to think of five positive things
that could possibly happen as a result of this problem.

There really is hope! God is "able to do immeasure-
ably more than all we ask or imagine, according to his
power that is at work within us" (Ephesians 3:20).

Yes, the trials of life are certainly painful. But by
remembering the truth that God is in control, we'll be
able to bounce back like Tammy . . . and like Joseph.

Nail It Down: Memorize Romans 8:28.

Pray About It:

FOUR

▼▼▼▼▼▼▼

Ross says: "A couple of days ago in the 'Work It Out' section, there was something about rejoicing when persecution comes. Yeah right! Somebody makes fun of me because I'm a Christian and I'm supposed to get excited about that? Give me a break!

"And before that you quoted a verse that says something like 'Consider it a joyful thing when trials come your way.' How could I be all joyful if, say, somebody rammed my new Jeep? Get real, dude!"

If you don't laugh, you'll cry!

Look It Up: It sounds hard to believe, but it really is possible to rejoice in the midst of problems. Here's why:

• Trials now—and our ability to keep trusting God in the midst of them—will result in heavenly reward later (James 1:12).

• Some trials prove that we are living the way the Lord wants us to live (2 Timothy 3:12).

• Trials don't cancel out God's past faithfulness or His future goodness. We can keep leaning on His promises.

Think It Through: A Chinese saying goes, "I was without shoes and complained. Then I met a man who had no feet." Many of the things that we consider huge trials—a pimple, one dateless weekend, flunking a quiz—are not big problems after all.

And even when the bottom really does fall out and you have to face a severe trial—serious illness, divorce, death in the family—remember that the God of all the universe loves you intensely and is with you constantly.

Work It Out: Take these steps to rejoicing in the midst of problems—

• List all the trials you face. Then list all the things you can thank God for. Which list is longer?

• Spend five minutes telling God how grateful you are for all the good things He has done, is doing, and will continue to do in your life.

• Thank God for your trials (1 Thessalonians 5:18), remembering that He will reward your faithfulness.

Have you taken all three of those steps? If so, you've just rejoiced in the midst of your trials!

Nail It Down: Read Acts 16:22-25. This weekend, read of the coming time when problems will end: On Saturday, Revelation 21; on Sunday, Revelation 22.

FIVE PROBLEMS

JESUS
What a Wild Dream!

Personal data: Kent Langston is 17, editor of the school paper, captain of the debate team, and a vocal agnostic. His goals are to get a college scholarship and become a rich journalist. His hobbies are tennis, reading science fiction, and making fun of Christians.

Circumstances: A long argument about Christianity with Laura Thornton (a debate team member who's a Christian) while eating pizza just before bedtime.

Outcome: The wildest dream you can imagine.

"In the beginning was the Word, and the Word was with God, and the Word was God. . . . The Word became flesh and made his dwelling among us" (John 1:1, 14).

K ent fought off his drowsiness. Laura Evans, "Miss Bible Banger" to Kent, had made him look stupid in front of his friends.

"I'll find mistakes in here if it takes all night," he thought, looking at his dusty New Testament. But as he read his eyelids got heavier and heavier.

Suddenly, Kent was standing on a street interviewing an ancient tax collector named Matthew.

"You're one of the people who followed Jesus. Who was He? A good teacher? A prophet? Or was He something more?"

Messiah via the book of Matthew

Look It Up: The bearded man smiled. "My response would be the same as Peter's when Jesus asked Him, 'Who do you say that I am?' "

"Simon Peter answered, 'You are the Christ, the Son of the living God' " (Matthew 16:16).

"See," Matthew continued, "In the Old Testament, God promised to send a 'Messiah' (the Hebrew word for 'Christ'). This One would be anointed as a king and priest to bring redemption and deliverance to His people. I wrote my gospel in order to show that Jesus is that Messiah promised in the Old Testament."

Think It Through: A lot of people think that Christ is simply Jesus' last name. Not so. It's a title—an awfully important one. It means that Jesus fulfilled all the Old Testament prophecies about the Messiah. Because He alone said and did things that the Christ would be able to say and do, we can know that Jesus is the Savior promised by God.

Work It Out: If you're Jewish and have never accepted Jesus as the Messiah, reread the prophecies in Isaiah 52 and 53. Then see how Jesus fits those descriptions of God's Anointed One by reading the book of Matthew in the New Testament.

Or maybe you're a Christian with Jewish friends. Write to Jews for Jesus, 60 Haight Street, San Francisco, CA 94102, for information on how to communicate with Jewish people the good news that Jesus is the Messiah.

Here's a prayer for the week: "Our Father, thank You for sending Christ to make us right with You. This week, as I tour quickly through the gospels, teach me more about Your Son, Jesus, in whose name I pray."

Nail It Down: Read Matthew 28:18-20.

✝ ✝ ✝ ✝ ✝ ✝ ✝ **ONE JESUS** ✝ ✝ ✝ ✝ ✝ ✝ ✝ ✝ ✝ ✝

The next thing Kent knew, he was playing tennis with Matthew, and running backward to return a lob shot. (Aren't dreams the weirdest?) And then without warning, he found himself sitting in a fishing boat with a friendly looking young man.

"You must be Kent, the journalist," the man said. "Hi. I'm Mark. Have you read my biography of Jesus?"

Kent rubbed his head. "What's going on here? I'm not even sure there is a God. Yet you Christians run all over the place saying, 'Not only does God exist, but this guy Jesus is Him!'"

Mark's message? A saving Servant

Look It Up: He grabbed Mark's collar, "Look, what's the story on this Jesus? Forget all that fairytale, miracle stuff in the Bible! I want the real scoop."

Mark looked right into his eyes, "Kent, I have written the absolute truth: Jesus is the all-powerful Savior of the world. My goal was to write a fast-moving account of His life that would demonstrate His mighty works and His mission of servanthood. That's why I included these words of Jesus:

"'Whoever wants to become great among you must be your servant, and whoever wants to be first must be slave of all. For even the Son of Man did not come to be served, but to serve, and to give his life as a ransom for many'" (Mark 10:43-45).

Think It Through: In Mark, Jesus is portrayed as a Servant, who constantly ministers to the physical and spiritual needs of others. Those who don't believe in Jesus miss out on more than eternal life in the future; they miss out on Jesus' fulfilling ministry in this life.

Jesus served others actively, compassionately, and sacrificially. Are you following His example?

Work It Out: Spend a minute looking at each of these incidents in the book of Mark: Jesus' encounter with the leper (1:40-45); His healing of the man with the shriveled hand (3:1-5); His feeding of the 5,000 (6:30-44). What do these incidents show you about Jesus' compassion and His willingness to serve?

Now, pick out a friend or neighbor who has physical or spiritual needs. Do something today—in the name of Christ— to help meet his or her needs.

Nail It Down: Read Mark 8:34-37.

Pray About It:

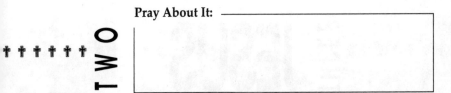

✝ ✝ ✝ ✝ ✝ ✝ T W O

As Kent and Mark were discussing Jesus, another man walked up. "That's Dr. Luke," Mark volunteered. "He also wrote an account of Christ's life."

"Good afternoon, gentlemen— And what, may I say, is that?" Dr. Luke questioned as he pointed at Kent's tennis racquet.

"It's used to hit a ball—in a game called tennis. Say, Dr. Luke, I'm really confused about this Jesus. Matthew says He's the Messiah. Mark here says He's a Servant. What do you think?"

At that, Mark turned into a fish, jumped into the water, and swam away. (What a dream!)

Looking at the Lord with Luke

Look It Up: "See you later, Mark," Dr. Luke called out. "Well, Kent, I guess I should tell you that I wasn't an eyewitness to all the events in my gospel. But don't worry your little agnostic head about that. I did plenty of detailed research. I interviewed many people who were followers of Christ. And I had the Holy Spirit directing me as I wrote.

"To answer your question, I'd say both Matthew and Mark are right. And I'm right too when I focus in my gospel on Christ the perfect Savior of mankind—Jews and Gentiles. He Himself said it best, 'The Son of Man came to seek and to save what was lost' " (Luke 19:10).

Think It Through: Christ's desire to save sinful men is stressed constantly in the book of Luke—especially in chapter 15. Note the reaction in heaven when a sinner turns to God (verses 7 and 10).

Just think: When a person trusts Jesus, there is a party in heaven!

Work It Out: Luke's biography of Christ includes personal snapshots—quick portraits of individuals that Jesus either met or talked about. Pick out a couple of these characters and list their positive and negative traits. If Luke had included a description of you in his gospel, what would he have said about you?

Pray this prayer: "Dear God, Thank You for sending Jesus, the perfect Savior. His compassion for people helps me see what kind of God You are—a forgiving and loving Heavenly Father. O Lord, help me to love You more and to walk closely with You today—just like your Son. Amen."

Nail It Down: Read Luke 24:45-48.

✝ ✝ ✝ ✝ ✝ ✝ ✝ **THREE JESUS** ✝ ✝ ✝ ✝ ✝ ✝ ✝ ✝ ✝ ✝

The dream con-
tinued. Kent
jumped into the
blue water for a
quick swim.
Suddenly a whale
swallowed him,
and within sec-
onds, spit him up
onto a deserted
beach. There, sit-
ting by a palm tree,
sat an old man
with white hair.

"Who are you?"
Kent asked rudely.

"I'm John, the
Apostle John. And
you must be Kent,
the young journal-
ist. And . . . wait,
don't tell me, you
must be here to ask
me some questions
about Jesus." (Kent
just stood there
with his jaw hang-
ing open.)

Jesus according to John

Look It Up: "Don't be surprised," the old man chuck-
led. "God showed me the end of the world in a vision.
Now here you are in Dream Land learning about His
Son."

Kent was speechless.

"I wrote my gospel to prove that Jesus is God in the
flesh, and that He proved it by the miracles He did."

John offered Kent an old scroll and said, "Jesus did
many other miraculous signs in the presence of his disciples, which are not recorded in this book. But these
are written that you may believe that Jesus is the Christ,
the Son of God, and that by believing you may have life
in his name" (John 20:30-31).

Think It Through: Why are there four gospels? Each
writer wrote from his own unique perspective.
- Matthew emphasized the words of the promised
  King;
- Mark stressed the works of the powerful Servant;
- Luke featured the humanity of the perfect Savior;
- John emphasized the Deity of the incarnate God.

Each gospel presents a different aspect of the life and
work of Christ. When we put them all together, we
have a complete picture of the Son of God!

Work It Out: When people read Matthew, Mark, Luke,
or John, they see Jesus Christ and are challenged to
believe in Him. What about when people read the
gospel according to you?

Think of an area in your life (your attitudes, conduct,
or speech) that may be keeping others from clearly seeing that Jesus is real. Admit to God that you need help in
that area and ask Him to help you change.

Nail It Down: Read John 1:1-18.

Pray About It:

FOUR

✝ ✝ ✝ ✝ ✝ ✝

The alarm clock-ended Kent's adventures in Dream Land.

But over the next few weeks he asked Laura a million questions. She answered some of them and a lot of times she simply said, "I'm not sure if anyone can tell you that." She gave Kent a copy of C. S. Lewis's *Mere Christianity*. He read that, and then he carefully read the four gospels of the New Testament.

Eight months after the dreams, Kent put his trust in Christ. He says, "There are a lot of side issues that I'm still not sure about, but I really believe that Jesus is who He said He is."

Kent's encounter with Christ

Look It Up: A lot of skeptics have turned away from God because of hypocritical Christians and/or the paradoxes of Christianity. Some, however, have later turned back to God because they couldn't escape the revealed truth of Christ. The Apostle Paul was such an individual.

"For you have heard of my previous way of life . . . how intensely I persecuted the church of God and tried to destroy it. . . . But when God, who set me apart from birth and called me by his grace, was pleased to reveal his Son in me . . . the churches of Judea . . . heard the report: 'The man who formerly persecuted us is now preaching the faith he once tried to destroy' " (Galatians 1:13-23).

Think It Through: The gospels are historical, but not merely historical. Their purpose is to elicit our response. We need to come to Christ in faith and receive the forgiveness and life that only He can offer. And we need to let the truth taught in the gospels propel us out into the world where we announce the Good News to others.

Work It Out: After some investigation, Kent trusted Jesus as his Savior. You can take that same step by sincerely praying: "Dear God, I'm a sinner who needs a relationship with You. Christ is the way to come back to You. Please forgive me and give me new life. Amen."

If you're already a believer in Christ, pick out a friend who needs to know the scoop about the Savior. Ask your friend questions today that will prompt a discussion about spiritual matters. Then simply share the facts: who Jesus is, what He did, why He did it, and what people need to do as a result.

Nail It Down: Read Colossians 1:13-20. On Saturday, read Psalm 22:1-21 for a prediction of the Cross. On Sunday, read Psalm 22:22-31 for a prediction of Christ's victory!

✝ ✝ ✝ ✝ ✝ ✝ ✝ FIVE JESUS ✝ ✝ ✝ ✝ ✝ ✝ ✝ ✝ ✝ ✝

HOLINESS

If you were playing the word association game and someone said the word *holiness*, what would you think of?

You'd probably associate holiness with *God*. But did you ever stop to think about what God's holiness really is? What does the Bible mean when it says , *"Holy, holy, holy is the LORD Almighty"* *(Isaiah 6:3)?*

The word translated "holy" in the Old Testament means "separated" or "cut apart." God is holy in that He is absolutely separate from everything He has created. He is a cut above everything in the universe. He is perfect, pure, separate from the slightest hint of error or evil.

We've played a word-association game; now let's play an imagination game. Try visualizing perfection. It isn't easy, is it? Try visualizing purity. That's just as difficult. But how are we to understand God's holiness if we can't picture what it means?

God provided a Way for us to understand Him, a model for us to picture. Jesus said, *"Anyone who has seen me has seen the Father"* *(John 14:9).* If we want to "see" the holiness of God more clearly, we need to look at the life of God's Son.

Jesus was holy in that He was perfect. He never made a mistake. He never miscalculated, misspoke, or misjudged. He always did the right thing at the right time in the right way. God is like that.

Jesus was holy in that He was pure. He never sinned (can you imagine that?). Yes, He walked among sinners. He mingled with them, ate with them, laughed with them, cried with them, healed them, and loved them. But He never became attached to their sinful attitudes or actions. And, with love, He called them to leave their lives of sin (John 8:11). God is like that.

But that's not all. The holy God expects us to be holy too: *"But just as he who called you is holy, so be holy in all you do; for it is written: 'Be holy, because I am holy' "* *(1 Peter 1:15-16).*

That's a tough standard—so tough that we'll never reach it in this life. But we can get closer to God's standard of holiness every day by following Christ. And we can rejoice that a day is coming when we too will stand in God's presence as holy people singing *"Holy, holy, holy is the LORD Almighty."*

CASH IT!

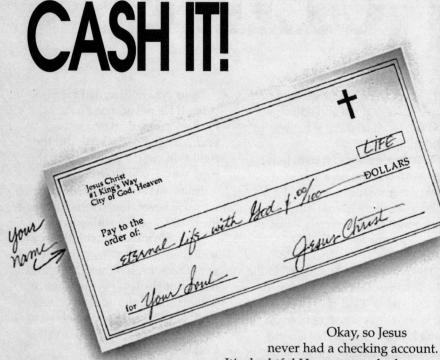

Jesus Christ
#1 King's Way
City of God, Heaven

Pay to the
order of: _____

Eternal life with God f.⁰⁰/₁₀₀ _____ DOLLARS

LIFE

for Your Soul

Jesus Christ

your name →

Okay, so Jesus never had a checking account. It's doubtful He ever even had any money. But still, look at all the financial transactions He made on behalf of a bankrupt human race:

He purchased Christians with his blood (1 Corinthians 6:19,20; Revelation 5:9).

He paid for the sins of the world (Romans 6:23; John 19:30; 1 John 2:2) with the riches of His grace (Ephesians 1:7).

He forgives our debts (Matthew 6:12).

He reserves treasure in heaven for His faithful followers (Luke 18:22).

To cash this check, all you have to do is believe He died for you and trust Him alone to make you acceptable to God.

The check is written and it's signed in blood, so cash it now. With Jesus' impending return, it might be difficult or even impossible to cash it tomorrow! Endorse Christ as your Savior now.

$$$$$$$$$$$ IDOLS $$$$$$$$$$$$$$$$$$
Where's God in Your Life?

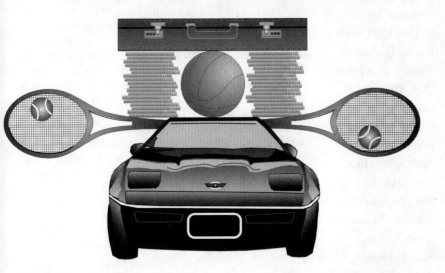

It's not just pagans in the jungle who are guilty. Or weird religious groups. Or people from centuries past. Christians today worship idols too.

Idolatry is the sin of getting caught up in something or so attached to someone that we let that thing or person replace God in our lives. This week we'll use God's Word to help us tear down five things that can easily become idols:

- Acceptance by friends
- Romantic relationships
- Music
- Success
- Material Goods

"Josiah removed all the detestable idols from all the territory . . . and he had all who were present . . . serve the LORD their God" (2 Chronicles 34:33).

$$

Taylor's living a double life . . . and it's about to drive him crazy. On Sunday he's a model Christian, singing all the hymns at church, listening to the sermons about Jesus Christ, and knowing deep-down in his heart that what he's hearing is true.

The rest of the week's a different story. When he's with his friends, the most popular group at school, his desire to be liked and accepted is so strong, he's even been doing some things he knows are dead wrong—heavy drinking on the weekends and heavy cheating in algebra class.

The powerful peer pressure god

Look It Up: Taylor is completely committed to the idol of being accepted by his friends. That, not God, is the most important thing in his life. He's not the first to struggle with this problem.

After Joshua led the Israelites into the Promised Land, he became concerned. Because Israel's new neighbors were not devoted to God, Joshua feared his countrymen might fall into the trap of worshipping their false gods. And so he challenged them, "If serving the LORD seems undesirable to you, then choose for yourselves this day whom you will serve. . . . But as for me and my house-hold, we will serve the LORD" (Joshua 24:15).

Three times the people vowed to serve God. But their desire to be accepted by their new neighbors was greater than their desire to please God. They got caught up in idolatry . . . with disastrous results (see Joshua 24:20 and Judges 2:11-23).

Think It Through: Can you think of some bad conse-quences that might result from Taylor's desiring accep-tance from his friends more than desiring God's approval?

Is it wrong to desire acceptance from our peers? Of course not. But when we want human approval more than Divine approval, we commit idolatry.

Work It Out: Here's how to tear down the totem pole of peer acceptance:
- Confess the ugly sin of idolatry (1 John 1:9).
- Dedicate yourself to God (Romans 12:1).
- Choose friends who will influence you to follow God, not your lusts (1 Corinthians 15:33).
- Dig deeply into God's Word to strengthen yourself against temptation (Psalm 119:9-11).

Nail It Down: Read Exodus 20:2-3.

$\$\$\$\$\$\$\$\$\$\$\$$ ONE IDOLS $\$\$\$\$\$\$\$\$\$\$\$\$\$$

Twelve months ago Becky was really excited about the Lord. She spent time with Him every day. She talked a lot about what He meant in her life. She was determined to please Him, no matter what. Everyone could tell He was more important to Becky than anything else.

Now, however, what excites Becky is Eric. She spends time with Eric every day. She talks non-stop about how much Eric means to her. It's obvious to everyone that Eric means more to Becky than anything or anyone—including God.

He's cute, but can he fulfill prayer?

Look It Up: Becky's committed to "The Religion of Romantic Relationships." Basically she has replaced the God of the Bible with Eric—the boyfriend god. Her situation isn't new. Even wise King Solomon of Israel got caught in the same trap.

Just like Becky, Solomon started out like gangbusters. He sincerely loved the Lord and eagerly sought God's wisdom. And God used him greatly. But then Solomon began to let romantic relationships rule his life. In complete disobedience to God's Word, he married hundreds of foreign woman with ungodly beliefs . . . with tragic results.

"As Solomon grew old, his wives turned his heart after other gods, and his heart was not fully devoted to the LORD his God, as the heart of David his father had been" (1 Kings 11:4).

Think It Through: What specific changes could Becky make in her relationship so that she's not guilty of idolatry? Is it only when a Christian dates a non-Christian that there is the danger of idolatry? Or is it possible for a Christian to also become obsessed with another Christian?

Remember, being in a dating relationship is not wrong—unless in our attitudes and actions we're more concerned with that person and more dedicated to him or her than we are to God.

Work It Out: See if you can come up with 5 danger signs, 5 indicators of an idolatrous dating relationship. List some of the possible ways Becky's idolatry might come back to haunt her.

Nail It Down: Read 1 Kings 11.

Pray About It:

$$$$$$$ TWO

139

Maybe you know someone like Matt. He's a music maniac. It's his whole life. Take a peek inside his bedroom (practically a music museum).

The walls and ceiling are plastered with posters. To the right is a $3,000 stereo system and a whole wall of albums, tapes, and compact discs. By the window is an electric guitar and a synthesizer. In the closet are T-shirts from each of the more than 100 concerts he's been to in the last couple of years. Matt's ultimate goal? To cut an album with his rap group, "What's it to ya"!

Matt's musical malfunction

Look It Up: Most teens don't succumb to music mania to the degree that Matt does. But let's face it—music is a big part of teenage life. Music, then, is an easy candidate for teen idolatry.

Each person must honestly examine his or her own heart and answer the big question, "Do I devote more time, attention, and concern to music than I do to the Lord?"

God's Word has a strong message for those who answer yes: "Therefore, my dear friends, flee from idolatry" (1 Corinthians 10:14).

Think It Through: Why do we get so caught up in the latest hit songs and the hottest new groups? What is it about music that makes millions of people spend billions of dollars each year to buy tapes and CDs and go to concerts? Why do more people watch the Grammy Awards than watch Billy Graham?

Would you rather see your favorite group in concert or spend a couple of hours learning how to study the Bible better? Could even contemporary Christian music be an idol in a person's life?

Work It Out: Do two experiments this week.
• Try to calculate how many hours a week you spend listening to the radio or to tapes and records. Then calculate how much time you spend in an average week praying or reading your Bible.
• Listen to the radio for half an hour. For every song you know the words to, memorize one Bible verse.

Nail It Down: Read 1 Thessalonians 1:9.

$$$$$$$$$$$ **THREE IDOLS** $$$$$$$$$$$$$$

Bruce and Peter are obsessed with the prospect of success—Bruce on the athletic field, Peter in the classroom.

They want to succeed so badly they can taste it. If Bruce can up his batting average and if Peter can maintain his 4.0 GPA, they'll probably both get scholarships.

Each has this attitude, "Hey, this is something I've worked my whole life for and I'm not gonna blow it now. Success means doing what it takes to get to the top. If some things have to slide well then, that's just the way it's got to be."

The secret of your success

Look It Up: The Bruces and Peters of the world need to know what God's Word says about success.

"Do not let this Book of the Law depart from your mouth; meditate on it day and night, so that you may be careful to do everything written in it. Then you will be prosperous and successful" (Joshua 1:8).

God is telling Joshua, the young leader of the Israelites, the secret to true success. Here it is: Real success comes when God's children obey His word!

Christians are not to forget God's commandments in order to achieve worldly success. That's idolatry! Rather, we are to focus on Him, obey the principles in His Word, and then work as hard as we can.

Think It Through: Peter and Bruce have an element of the truth in their thinking. Yes, success is usually the result of hard work toward a goal. (The Biblical term for that concept is "faithfulness.") And yes, it's a good thing, even an admirable thing, to work hard to be a good athlete or good student.

But here's where Peter and Bruce go wrong: Their success means more to them than God. Their idol can't be seen, smelled, tasted, touched, or heard. But to God, it's as sinful as the golden calf Moses destroyed.

Work It Out: In what areas are you tempted to pursue success more than God? If God has gifted you and granted you success in athletics, academics, business, making friends, the arts, or any other area, stop right now and give Him thanks.

And make sure you prove your gratefulness to Him by keeping your gifts and goals in proper perspective.

Nail It Down: See the source of real success in Nehemiah 2:20.

Pray About It:

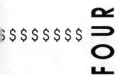

$$$$$$$ FOUR

M ingle with the crowd at Dale's Friday night party.

Out front is Steve in his new Miata, impressing a crowd of admirers with his car's AM/FM stereo CD player.

In the living room as several girls rave about Stephanie's new $400 outfit, one whispers, "She's got enough clothes to open her own mall!"

In the kitchen, John, the popular but overweight class clown, is finishing off the contents of Dale's refrigerator.

And Kris, the cutest and best school cheerleader, is in the bathroom for the fourth time, checking her hair and make-up.

Living in a material world

Look It Up: Dale's party is a good place to see some of the things that can become idols in our lives.

About cars and clothes, remember: "Every good and perfect gift is from above, coming down from the Father of the heavenly lights" (James 1:17). Don't begin to value created things more than the Creator!

About food, remember that God's Word condemns gluttony—being controlled by one's appetite (Philippians 3:19). Concentrate on spiritual as well as physical food.

About appearance, remember that God doesn't see us the way we see each other (1 Samuel 16:7). Focus on how you look on the inside as well as on the outside.

Think It Through: An idol is anything that comes to be more important to us than God.

The things we've looked at this week—friendships, dating relationships, music, success, cars, clothes, food, and appearance—are not always idols. They only become idols or false gods when we place more emphasis on them than we do on our relationship with God. We can enjoy all those things without guilt as long as God remains our ultimate priority.

Work It Out: Check for idols in your life by answering these questions: What do I think about most? How do I spend my free time? If someone closely examined my life, what would he or she say was most important to me?

You can tear down any idols you find by confessing your sin and changing your actions. Act quickly to make the Lord No. 1 in your life. Ask Him for the strength to overcome the idolatrous temptations all around you.

Nail It Down: Read Isaiah 2:12-18. On Saturday, read Romans 1. On Sunday, memorize Romans 1:25.

$$\$\$\$\$\$\$\$\$\$\$\$ \quad \text{F I V E} \quad \textbf{IDOLS} \quad \$\$\$\$\$\$\$\$\$\$\$\$\$\$\$$

142

╪╪╪╪╪╪╪╪╪╪╪╪╪ FAITH ╪╪╪╪╪╪╪╪╪╪╪╪╪╪╪╪╪
What Do You Believe?

"The righteous will live by his faith" (Habakkuk 2:4).

Faith. It's one of those concepts like justice or truth that you perhaps vaguely understand, but find hard to explain to others.

The dictionary says faith is "belief not based on proof or evidence." But is that what Biblical faith really means? Is it putting your brain on the shelf? Does a believer have to kiss reason and common sense good-bye?

Check out the following pages to see:

- What is Biblical faith?
- What common errors or problems hinder true faith?
- How can I increase weak faith?
- Are what I believe (faith) and what I do (works) related?
- How should faith affect my everyday life?

╪╪

Here are two speakers at the same youth conference using almost identical words. Are they saying the same thing?

Speaker #1: "Young people, if you want to have your sins forgiven and to go to heaven, the Bible says that you need to believe that Jesus Christ died on the cross for your sins and that He rose again. That's what faith is—believing the gospel."

Speaker #2: "Young people, if you want to have your sins forgiven and to go to heaven, you need to believe in Jesus. That's what faith is—trusting in the Lord Jesus Christ."

Figuring out what faith really is

Look It Up: Well, is faith believing that (agreeing to the facts) or is it believing in (trusting in a person)?
- "If you do not believe that I am the one I claim to be, you will indeed die in your sins" (John 8:24).
- "For my Father's will is that everyone who looks to the Son and believes in him shall have eternal life" (John 6:40).

From just these two verses—we could look at dozens of others—faith appears to consist of both parts: believing the facts about Christ and turning away from our sins and toward Him in personal trust.

Think It Through: A top-notch repairman finishes working on an elevator on the 50th floor of an office building. He then says to the two men watching him, "Climb aboard, guys. She's all fixed up, good as new."

The first man says, "I believe that's an elevator, and I believe you repaired it, but . . . get in? No thanks, I don't trust you enough." The man then takes the stairs.

The second man says to the repairman, "I recognize you. You maintain the elevators in our building, and they always work properly. No problem." He steps inside.

Work It Out: Find an index card and write across the top of it "My Faith." Draw a line down the center of the card from top to bottom, making two columns. At the top of the column on the left, write: "Strong." At the top of the column on the right, write: "Weak."

Today, list your acts of strong faith in the "Strong" column and acts of weak faith in the "Weak" column.

At the end of the day, evaluate your faith. Is your faith like the first or the second man's faith? Is your faith strong enough—or too weak—to produce actions?

Nail It Down: Read James 2:14-17.

ONE FAITH

144

Charles says, "I think sincerity is as important as faith. I know a Mormon family whose devotion to God puts mine to shame. Can I look at them and say, 'Your faith is false'? I feel like God is going to say to them, 'Well, at least you were sincere.'"

Cheryl says: "Faith is a pretty shaky deal, don't you think? In other words, you hope all these things about God are true. But you can't know for sure. I mean, after all, you've never seen Him."

Are all forms of faith okay?

Look It Up: When it comes to a subject as crucial as faith, God doesn't want us guessing or relying on our own opinions. Consider these verses:

• "I have declared to both Jews and Greeks that they must turn to God in repentance and have faith in our Lord Jesus" (Acts 20:21). Notice that true faith must be in Jesus, not in sincerity or another religion.

• "Now faith is being sure of what we hope for and certain of what we do not see" (Hebrews 11:1). Notice that faith is not wishful thinking. True faith is "being sure" that what God has said will come to pass.

Think It Through: Has Cheryl ever seen gravity? No, but she has seen its effects. And so, she has faith that gravity exists. But if invisibility isn't enough to shake Cheryl's faith in gravity, why does it shake her faith in God?

What if Charles's Mormon friend put wings on a tricycle and seriously believed that it could fly across the Atlantic Ocean? Would he get wet? Obviously. True faith requires more than mere sincerity.

Work It Out: When you hear your friends saying things like: "All you have to do is be sincere in your beliefs," ask them, "If a person sincerely believed an elephant could fly, would that mean an elephant could truly fly?"

When someone says to you: "Everybody's beliefs are true," ask them, "Does that mean Jesus' belief that He is the only way to heaven (John 14:6) is true?" If they say no, then remind them that even they don't really think everybody's beliefs are true. If they say yes, ask them: "Then why don't you put your faith in Him?"

Nail It Down: Read Romans 3:22.

Pray About It:

+++++++ T W O

There's a discussion about faith going on in the 11th-grade religion class at Wesley Academy. Everyone's got something to say (mostly about how little faith they have):

Peggy: "With all the bad stuff going on in my life right now, my faith is just about gone."

Roy: "Yeah, me too. At church we always hear about these missionaries and great men of faith. I can't relate to that! I have a hard enough time just believing in God, much less that He cares about me and wants to 'use me in a powerful way.'"

Improving a weak faith

Look It Up: Do doubts attack your faith in the same way that the Arnold Schwarzenegger-built beach bully kicked sand in the face of the 98-pound weakling? You don't have to put up with that kind of treatment.

• Time in the Word can make your faith grow. "Consequently, faith comes from hearing the message, and the message is heard through the word of Christ" (Romans 10:17).

• The Lord can strengthen a weak faith (Mark 9:21-27).

• Even a little faith—if it is placed in the Person of Christ—can produce powerful results (Luke 17:5-6)!

Think It Through: Suppose you were going steady with someone, but your boy or girlfriend didn't contact you for a month. Would you still feel confident about the relationship? Probably not. You'd likely begin to wonder what was up. You'd probably be bombarded by doubts.

In the same way, if we're not reading the Bible on a regular basis, hearing what God wants to say to us, we forget His presence, power, and love. We get fearful and our faith begins to crumble.

Work It Out: Give your faith muscles a regular work-out, beginning today. Be reminded of God's greatness and power by spending a few extra minutes each day in God's Word.

Besides reading the verses that are printed out in the "Look It Up" sections of this devotional, make sure you look up the Scripture references that are also listed. And don't forget the additional passages that are mentioned in the "Nail It Down" sections.

Feeding on the the Word of God will build up your spiritual muscles.

Nail It Down: Read 2 Thessalonians 1:3.

+++++++++++ THREE **FAITH** +++++++++++++++++++

In Sunday school or at youth group, Liz can give all the right answers. She can talk about her faith all day and quote Bible verses about the way Christians are supposed to live. But get her away from church, and her lifestyle is anything but Christian.

Becky, on the other hand, couldn't begin to tell you what she believes! The Bible isn't a book she normally reads, and her church basically just keeps telling her to do good deeds for everybody. So off she goes, working like crazy, trying hard to be a "good Christian."

True faith results in good works

Look It Up: As you probably have already guessed, neither of the above extremes is healthy. The Bible is clear on two points:

1. We're saved from sin and death through faith, not deeds. "For it is by grace you have been saved, through faith—and this not from yourselves, it is the gift of God—not by works, so that no one can boast" (Ephesians 2:8-9).

2. Genuine faith results in good deeds. "What good is it, my brothers, if a man claims to have faith but has no deeds? Can such faith save him?" (James 2:14).

Think It Through: For centuries, Bible scholars have argued about the connection between faith and good deeds. The whole issue becomes clear when you realize that we are saved by faith alone; however, good deeds are the outcome of real faith. Deeds prove—not produce—saving faith.

Are you like Liz? Like Becky?

Work It Out: Does either of these statements describe you: "I'm all talk and no action" or "I'm trying to work my way into heaven"? If so, here's how to find a genuine faith.

First, make sure that you have truly believed. Second, put your faith into practice by doing what God's Word says. Show kindness to a family member or neighbor. Help someone in trouble. Give your time and resources. In short, meet every need that comes your way that you are capable of meeting.

That's what Christ did. And that's what Christians are to do.

Nail It Down: Read Hebrews 11 to see how faith is always connected with doing something.

Pray About It:

FOUR

+·+·+·+·+·+·+·+·+

All week Amy has been reading about what it really means to believe. She's thought about the connection between faith and good deeds. She probably knows more about what the Bible says about faith than 90 percent of her friends. But still she has some questions.

"It just seems so vague. I know I am saved by faith. But how does faith affect my day-to-day Christian life? Does it really make a difference?"

How faith affects your everyday life

Look It Up: Glad you asked, Amy. Look at this verse:

"So then, just as you received Christ Jesus as Lord, continue to live in him" (Colossians 2:6).

In essence, Paul is saying this: "You trusted in Christ to forgive your sins and to make you right with God by faith, right? Now, as a Christian, keep on living by faith all the time. Keep taking Christ at His Word. Don't depend on your own power to live the Christian life. And don't depend on your own judgments. Instead, depend on Christ. He lives in you through the Spirit, and He has spoken His judgments to you in His Word."

Think It Through: Faith isn't just momentary belief that guarantees heaven and stops at the moment of salvation. And faith isn't a feeling that comes and goes. Faith is recognizing: "God said it. I believe it and choose to act on it." Faith means trusting His Word (regardless of circumstances or feelings) and letting Him work in and through you in every situation everyday.

Work It Out: Want some concrete ways to demonstrate faith? Read on. (And remember, you asked for it!)

Depend on God to give you a love for that person you can't stand, to give you His strength to face a severe trial, to give you a vision and a plan to reach your school for Christ this next year.

Ask God for opportunities to share the gospel, for discipline to meet all your obligations, for new friendships, for growth in your youth group, for a greater hunger for His Word, for creative ways to improve things at home, for a stronger character in your own life. (And believe that He will grant your requests!)

Nail It Down: Read 2 Corinthians 5:7. On Saturday read John 15:5. On Sunday read Philippians 2:12-13.

+++++++++++ FIVE **FAITH** ++++++++++++++++++

DESTINY
Where Are You Headed?

Once upon a time, people believed in heaven and hell. The general consensus was, "Heaven is the place to shoot for. You want to end up there. Hell? Uh, that's another story."

Now, however, people are "sophisticated." To believe in the reality of either destiny is, in the minds of "enlightened" individuals, as silly as believing in the tooth fairy and the Easter bunny.

Why then did Jesus and His followers talk so much about each place?

"Unless your righteousness surpasses that of the Pharisees and the teachers of the law, you will certainly not enter the kingdom of heaven. . . . Anyone who says, 'You fool!' will be in danger of the fire of hell" Matthew 5:20, 22).

Yesterday Tim Morris's mom told the senior high Sunday school class about the strange experience she had when her heart stopped during surgery.

"I realized I was looking down at the doctors working on me. Just then, I felt a warm breeze gently pushing my soul through a long dark tunnel. In seconds I was in a room filled with dazzling light and beautiful music. Straight ahead on a massive, golden throne sat a man in glowing robes. Figures in white were walking toward me. All of a sudden, my mind went blank."

Mortals will move into immortality

Look It Up: Whether such experiences are real or imaginary is hard to say. But two things are certain:

1. This present life will one day cease for all of us (Hebrews 9:27).

2. Every person will exist somewhere for eternity.

Jesus emphasized these truths when he told the story of the rich man (traditionally known as "Dives") and Lazarus. Poor Lazarus died and was carried by angels to Paradise. "The rich man also died.... In hell, where he was in torment, he looked up and saw Abraham far away, with Lazarus by his side" (Luke 16:22-23).

The story, besides reminding us that all—rich and poor alike—die, shows that death is not the end. We are immortal creatures with specific destinies.

Think It Through: Few people think about death. We prefer to believe that things will always go on as they are. But make no mistake: You will depart from this world.

Think about these words of C. S. Lewis: "There are no ordinary people. You have never talked to a mere mortal. ... It is immortals whom we joke with, work with, marry, snub, and exploit—immortal horrors or everlasting splendors" (The Weight of Glory).

Work It Out: Live today like it is your last day on earth. (It might very well be!) Don't turn off your brain and heart and coast through life. Listen to people. Observe God's magnificent creation. Think about things that matter—loving God and showing others His love.

Treat the people around you like the immortal creatures they are. Each one will spend eternity either with God or apart from God.

That's a sobering fact. Try to keep it in mind today.

Nail It Down: Read Daniel 12:2.

⇕ ⇕ ⇕ ⇕ ⇕ ⇕ ⇕ ONE DESTINY ⇕ ⇕ ⇕ ⇕ ⇕ ⇕ ⇕

Seven juniors — three guys and four girls—are sitting at a picnic table during lunch. They talk about snowskiing, why anybody would want to eat vienna sausages, and hell. (Don't ask how they got from vienna sausages to hell; you wouldn't believe it!)

Doug: "C'mon, Gretchen, you don't really believe that, do you? A place where people burn forever?"

Sue: "Really. If there even is a God, I doubt if He's cruel enough to send people somewhere like that."

The reality we'd like to forget

Look It Up: Hell is not a pleasant topic. People would rather pretend it doesn't exist. Yet according to the Bible
* Hell is real (Matthew 5:29-30);
* Hell is horrible. It is likened to a place of burning and fire (Matthew 5:22; Mark 9:42-48); darkness and weeping (Matthew 8:11,12); torment (Revelation 14:9-11); and wrath (John 3:36). It is also described as a dungeon (2 Peter 2:4); a furnace (Matthew 13:40-42); and a lake of burning sulfur (Revelation 19:20).
* Hell is eternal. "He will punish those who do not know God and do not obey the gospel of our Lord Jesus. They will be punished with everlasting destruction and shut out from the presence of the Lord and from the majesty of his power" (2 Thessalonians 1:8-9).

Think It Through: According to Matthew 25:41, God created hell as a place of judgment for Satan and the other angels who rebelled against God. (See Isaiah 14:12-20 and Ezekiel 28:14-19.) But since mankind sinned against God too, hell also includes unrepentant humans. God is holy and just and must punish sin.

Jesus talked a lot more about hell than about heaven. To say hell is merely a myth is to say that Jesus believed and taught what we now know are primitive myths.

Work It Out: Here's a prayer for today: "Father, cause the truth about hell to sink into my head and heart. Give me compassion for people who are headed to hell because they don't know You."

At lunch today or tomorrow, bring up the topic of hell and see what happens. Many people are more willing to hear about Christ when they finally understand the reality of hell.

Nail It Down: Read Matthew 25:31-46.

Pray About It: _____

↕ ↕ ↕ ↕ ↕

T W O

151

The time: Saturday afternoon about 4:30.

The activity: Watching a movie called, "Heaven Can Wait" on television.

The command: "Go rake the backyard ... now!"

The plan: Try to make an unpleasant job more endurable. So ... Norm brings his radio-cassette player out on the back porch and cranks it up loud enough to melt your face off.

The songs: A bunch of new stuff, plus two older songs —John Lennon singing "Imagine there's no heaven ..." followed by Belinda Carlisle singing "Heaven is a Place on Earth."

What is heaven really like?

Look It Up: There have been countless references to heaven in music and numerous portrayals of heaven in movies and literature. Are these descriptions accurate? What is heaven really like?

The Bible says heaven is
• a place where the Triune God (1 Kings 8:30; Psalm 103:19) and His angels (Matthew 18:10) dwell, and where believers in Christ will live for eternity (2 Corinthians 5:6-8; Philippians 1:21-23);
• a place of beauty (Revelation 21:1–22:5);
• a place of perfection: "He will wipe every tear from their eyes. There will be no more death or mourning or crying or pain. ... Nothing impure will ever enter it. ... No longer will there be any curse. ... There will be no more night" (Revelation 21:4, 27; 22:3, 5).

Think It Through: Think of the most beautiful place you've ever seen. Think of the happiest you've ever been. Try to remember when you felt closest to God. Imagine living with no problems. Imagine the perfect house in the perfect city. Multiply it all by an infinite number and you still won't match the bliss contained in heaven's greatest promise: seeing God face-to-face.

Work It Out: Make a list of all the songs, plays, movies, short stories, poems, and TV shows you can think of that make reference to heaven. Are these descriptions based on the truth of Scripture or on human speculation?

Do a survey with some of your friends and/or family members today. Ask them if they believe in heaven and if so, what they think it is going to be like. You'll be guaranteed an interesting conversation.

Nail It Down: Read about Isaiah's glimpse of heaven— Isaiah 6:1-8.

↕↕↕↕↕↕↕↕ **THREE DESTINY** ↕↕↕↕↕↕↕↕↕

Jenny asks the question that everyone else is thinking:

"Heaven sounds, well, okay, don't get mad at me for saying this—but heaven sounds . . . boring. I mean, I know it'll probably be beautiful and everything —diamonds and gold and stuff. But what are we going to do there? If all you do is like sit around and sing, then that sounds to me like going to church for eternity. And church isn't always that fun. And heaven is supposed to be a place where we'll be happy, right?"

But what will we do in heaven?

Look It Up: Good question, Jenny. What are we going to do in heaven? Well, according to the Bible we will:
- Rest (Revelation 14:13).
- Fellowship with other believers (Revelation 19:7-9).
- Know God perfectly (Revelation 21:3; 22:4).
- Worship God (Revelation 19:1-8).
- Serve God. "The throne of God and of the Lamb will be in the city, and his servants will serve him" (Revelation 22:3).
- Reign with God. "And they will reign for ever and ever" (Revelation 22:5).

Think It Through: Have you ever met someone and thought, "Yuck!" only to find out later that you had been totally wrong about that person?

It's that way with God sometimes. He gets a lot of bad press. For thousands of years now, people have been spreading rumors that He's mean, boring, and not someone with whom you want to get too involved.

Wrong! Knowing God (when you see what He's really like) is the greatest joy in life. And living with Him in heaven will be the ultimate in excitement!

Work It Out: It's not clear how believers will serve God and reign with Him for all eternity. Will we zoom around the universe in glorified, resurrected bodies (Philippians 3:21)? Will we govern other planets in the new heaven and new earth (Revelation 21:1)? Only God knows.

What is clear is that our actions now determine our heavenly role later! (see Matthew 25:14-30) With that in mind, get back to basics today: In every situation you face, ask yourself, "What would God have me to do?" Then do it—out of love for God and for your fellow man.

Nail It Down: Read Revelation 22:12-14.

Pray About It:

⇕ ⇕ ⇕ ⇕ ⇕ ⇕ **FOUR**

153

Shawn went with a friend on a church youth retreat last weekend. She had fun, but something the speaker said Sunday morning is still bugging her five days later.

He asked the question, "If you died today, do you know for sure where you would spend eternity?"

All week Shawn has been wrestling with that question. She wants to get the issue settled in her mind, but she doesn't know where to find the answer.

Do you know where you'll go?

Look It Up: Talking about this issue of personal destiny, Jesus said:

• "Whoever believes in him [the Son of God] is not condemned, but whoever does not believe stands condemned already" (John 3:18).

• "I tell you the truth, whoever hears my word and believes him who sent me has eternal life and will not be condemned; he has crossed over from death to life" (John 5:24).

Paul said, "The gift of God is eternal life in Christ Jesus our Lord" (Romans 6:23).

Notice that this gift of eternal life is, according to Jesus, for "whoever believes."

Think It Through: This week we've seen that (1) every person on this planet will spend eternity somewhere; (2) hell is a horrible place where unbelievers will end up; (3) heaven is that magnificent place where God dwells and believers will enter; (4) in heaven believers will serve and worship God, and reign with Him forever.

The big question is, "Do you know your destiny?"

Work It Out: You can know for sure where you will spend eternity. If you have truly trusted Jesus Christ to forgive your sins, God's Word guarantees you eternal life with God in heaven (John 3:16).

If you have never trusted Christ, you need to do so now. Talk to God in prayer and tell Him that you are a sinner— you've broken His law. Tell Him that you want Christ's death on the cross to pay for your sin. Then ask Him to change your life. That's a request He will answer!

Nail It Down: Read 1 John 5:11-13. On Saturday read a description of the doomed: Revelation 21:8. On Sunday read a description of the redeemed: Revelation 7:9-10.

↕ ↕ ↕ ↕ ↕ ↕ ↕   FIVE **DESTINY** ↕ ↕ ↕ ↕ ↕ ↕ ↕

THE MESSAGE OF THE BIRDS

Despite a godly wife and Christian kids, the middle-aged farmer was skeptical about matters of religion and faith. He had vowed as a young man never to attend church. He had kept that vow for more than 30 years.

So on December 24, the story goes, when the rest of the family headed out into the snow for a special Christmas Eve service, the farmer stayed home.

In a few minutes the man was startled by an irregular bumping sound. Upon investigating he realized the noise was due to a flock of tiny sparrows that were repeatedly flying into the warm room's picture window.

Moved to compassion, the farmer went out into the cold night. He opened the barn door, turned on the building's lights, and left a trail of bread crumbs leading inside. But the birds scattered into the frigid darkness.

The farmer tried other tactics—circling behind the sparrows and attempting to shoo them inside, whistling at them, going in and out of the house. But nothing worked. The terrified birds couldn't grasp that the man was only trying to help. To them, he was just an alien creature.

In frustration the farmer finally retreated into his house. He watched the doomed sparrows for a long time through the front window. As he pondered their plight, the thought hit him like a bolt of lightning: "If only I could become a bird for just a moment. Then I wouldn't frighten them. Then I could show them the way to safety."

In the next instant, as church bells began chiming in the distance, the farmer was struck by another thought: "Now I understand the faith of my family. This Jesus they love, worship, and serve, was God become man! He took on flesh to offer scared and dying people safety and life."

With tears in his eyes the farmer pulled a dusty Bible off the shelf, sat down in front of the fireplace, and began to read.

INCARNATION

When you think of Christmas, the word *Incarnation* probably isn't the first idea that comes to your mind. But when you celebrate Christmas each year, you are actually celebrating the Incarnation of Christ, a truth which was revealed to us by His birth.

Jesus is God *incarnate*. God was made into flesh—the same flesh of which we are made. This is one of the most basic doctrines of our faith. It is what makes Christianity different from any other religion. In no other religion does God come to live on earth as a human being. This is why Jesus is called "Immanuel," which in Hebrew means "God with us."

The first person to receive the news of Christ's Incarnation was His mother-to-be, Mary. Since she was a virgin, she did not understand how she could become the mother of Christ, but willingly accepted God's promise that *"the holy one to be born will be called the Son of God"* (Luke 1:35).

The fact that Jesus' mother was an earthly woman shows that He is human. The fact that she was a virgin shows unmistakably that He is the Son of God. Because He was begotten of God, whereas we are begotten of man, He inherits the Father's divinity.

God did not choose to come to us as some extra-terrestrial alien. He had a birth, was raised in a family, and learned how to be a carpenter like His earthly father. He got hungry, got dirty, and went to sleep at night. He felt great love for His friends and great pain when He was betrayed by them. Hebrews 2:18 tells us that Jesus understands and identifies with all of our difficulties in living a life pleasing to God: *"Because He himself suffered when he was tempted, he is able to help those who are being tempted."*

Just as Jesus is fully human, He is fully divine—fully God. He never left anyone in doubt about this: *"I came from the Father and entered the world"* (John 16:28). His purpose on earth was to give His life as a payment for our sins that we might be forgiven. And if His life was to be an acceptable payment, it had to be totally free of sin. God knew that no man's life was, or ever would be, free of sin. The only possible way He could save us was to give part of His own life.

We can put our full trust in everything Jesus taught or did because we know He is God. We can know and love Him personally as our friend and brother because He is a Man.

That is fantastic news! Have you told anyone lately what the Incarnation means to you?

CHARACTER
Qualities of a Christian

All the students in Mrs. Lansing's second-period English class are writing furiously.

For them, it's an essay on "The Person I Admire Most and Why." For us, it's a chance to examine qualities we need to develop in our own lives.

For them, the goal is simple: a decent grade in English composition. For us, the goal is a little more complex: an A in Character 101.

Sharpen your pencils.

"Be imitators of God"
(Ephesians 5:1).

Russell got Mrs. Lansing's assignment mixed up. Instead of writing about a person, he's describing a trait: "Loyalty is what I admire the most in a person. The dictionary says loyalty means being faithful to a person, cause, or ideal. It means you can be counted on or depended on. A loyal person is a committed person.

"When I hear the word loyal, I immediately think of General Norman Schwartzkopf. He showed loyalty to the President and to the country. When I watched him on television, I got the feeling that he would do anything for his country. That's loyalty."

Loyal as the general

Look It Up: Loyalty is a rarity. People change jobs, spouses, churches, and friends without a moment's thought. Is loyalty a character quality Christians should possess? Yes!

Ever heard of Onesiphorus? (How would you like a name like that?) Onesiphorus (we'll call him "O" for short) was a friend of Paul's.

When Paul was in prison for his Christian beliefs, "O" happened on the scene. Most of Paul's friends had deserted him, but not "O"! He risked his own neck (literally!) to come and minister to Paul. The apostle writes in his last letter, "Onesiphorus . . . was not ashamed of my chains. On the contrary, when he was in Rome, he searched hard for me until he found me" (2 Timothy 1:16-17).

Now that's loyalty!

Think It Through: Real loyalty survives difficult times. Real loyalty can cost you a lot—your job, your reputation, your friendships, sometimes even your safety or your life.

But doesn't anything really worth having cost a lot?

Imagine that you're in the audience of the Sally Jessy Raphael show when her guest is a scholar who says the Bible is a backward book of silly myths.

How could you show your loyalty to God?

Work It Out: Think of someone in your life who needs a "Stormin' Norman" right now—someone who really needs a friend.

Show your loyalty by
• writing a note;
• paying a visit;
• giving a hug; or
• just listening to your needy friend.
They'll never forget your kindness—or you!

Nail It Down: Meditate on John 15:13.

◆◆◆◆◆◆◆ **ONE CHARACTER** ◆

Jan stared blankly out the window. "I don't know who to write about," she thought. Then as she rubbed a bruise on her knee, an idea came. She began:

"The person I admire most is my Aunt Katherine. She's had surgery on both knees about 15 times. Three years ago my Uncle Bill died. Now she's all alone. A year ago, she lost one of her legs.

"You'd think all this would make her mad at God. But she still has her faith and she still loves life. She's an amazing woman, my Aunt Katherine. I admire her ability to keep at it."

How to run in the marathon of life

Look It Up: Endurance is the ability to hang in there during hard times. It's standing firm under suffering, stress, and trials. Endurance is an admirable trait in anyone, but it's an expected trait in Christians. A good example in the Bible of endurance is in the life of the Apostle Paul.

While trying to take the good news of God's love to the world, he was beaten, whipped, imprisoned, shipwrecked, and stoned. He went without food, and sleep (see 2 Corinthians 11:23-27).

But he never quit, because he was aware that God rewards endurance: "Let us not become weary in doing good, for at the proper time we will reap a harvest if we do not give up" (Galatians 6:9).

Think It Through: Don't you think there must have been times when Paul felt like throwing in the towel? If you were in a similar situation, do you think you would endure those things for Christ? Why do you think that many Christians, when persecuted or undergoing suffering, seem to get stronger?

There's no magic formula for endurance. Just look to God for His strength and grace and then live by the facts of His Word, not by your feelings (2 Corinthians 5:7).

Work It Out: Do you ever feel like quitting because of hard times? Share those struggles with your parents, youth leader, or a close friend. Sometimes, endurance comes easier if we have someone who will walk alongside us.

If you know people who are suffering or hurting, try to help them endure. Think of ways you could help make their rough times a little smoother.

Then do it today!

Nail It Down: Read 2 Timothy 2:3.

Pray About It:

T W O

Sandra starts writing her essay right away.

"My mom is the greatest lady in the world. I hope I turn out like her. She's a great listener. She trusts me. Plus she likes to do all kinds of fun stuff.

"Most of all, I admire her compassion. If anybody is in trouble, or hurt, she goes way out of her way to help. Once mom organized the ladies at church to round up clothes and food for tornado victims. When she sees little kids in wheelchairs she starts crying! It's kind of embarrassing. But she really cares."

Compassion is always in fashion

Look It Up: For the world's best example of compassion, open your Bible to the gospels.

Never has anyone been so moved by the needs of people and done so much to meet those needs as Jesus Christ. Look at these examples:

"When he saw the crowds, he had compassion on them, because they were harassed and helpless, like sheep without a shepherd" (Matthew 9:36).

"When Jesus . . . saw a large crowd, he had compassion on them and healed their sick" (Matthew 14:14).

Think It Through: God's goal is that His children become just like Jesus Christ. This means we must ask Jesus to express His compassion in and through us. Our hands and feet become His—and He is then able to use us to show His compassion to a hurting world.

Would Christ make fun of someone who tripped and fell? Would He snicker at a friend in trouble? Would He walk away from anyone who needed and wanted help?

Work It Out: Think of some specific ways you could show compassion to the following people:
- a friend who discovers she's pregnant;
- someone who drops his tray in front of 500 people in the lunchroom;
- a person who's being mocked because of the way she looks or dresses;
- a classmate whose parents are splitting up;
- someone who just lost a loved one.

So many people are hurting all around you today. Ask Jesus Christ to minister His compassion through you.

Nail It Down: Memorize Colossians 3:12.

✦✦✦✦✦✦✦✦ THREE CHARACTER ✦

Ricardo has only been in this country for seven years. His family came from Mexico. He's a hardworking, popular student who wants to become a journalist. He writes:

"My hero is Geraldo Rivera. Even though he is a member of a minority, he has become highly successful at what he does. His live documentaries have focused a lot of attention on some of America's biggest problems.

"Geraldo is bold. I don't agree with him all the time, but he's not afraid to confront people with their crimes. I'd like to be that fearless when I become a reporter."

Be bold—break the mold!

Look It Up: The Bible is full of men and women who were bold for God. Take the Apostle Peter for instance.

When the first-century church was just coming into existence, Christians faced opposition and persecution from both religious and political leaders. As the leader of the church, Peter might have been tempted to think, "We'd better not rock the boat. We can believe in Jesus, but let's just sort of keep it to ourselves. After all, a person's faith is between him and God."

But he didn't! With a deep faith in God, and empowered by the Holy Spirit, Peter boldly shared the Good News of Jesus Christ with whomever would listen.

And when arrested and ordered to stop witnessing, Peter and John replied, " 'Judge for yourselves whether it is right in God's sight to obey you rather than God. For we cannot help speaking about what we have seen and heard' " (Acts 4:19-20).

Think It Through: Boldness doesn't mean being rude or obnoxious. What are some ways a Christian can stand up for Christ without turning everyone off?

Boldness does mean being confident. The better we understand God's love, power, and protection in our lives, the bolder we'll become.

Work It Out: Follow these steps for more boldness in your walk with the Lord:

• remember that God is the awesome Lord of all the universe—and therefore in control of your circumstances;

• make sure you're living a life pleasing to God;

• ask God to make you bold. (Since God wants you to be bold, don't you think He'll answer that prayer?)

Nail It Down: Read Acts 5:25-29.

Pray About It: —————————

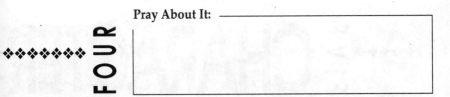

❖❖❖❖❖❖❖

F O U R

161

Christi's essay begins like this:

"I look up to a number of people in life. But the person I most respect and admire is my dad.

"My dad is a successful businessman and a leader in the church. He coaches Little League baseball and makes the best blueberry pancakes ever. But If I had to pick one word to describe my dad it would be dependable. He's always there for me. If he makes a promise or says he's going to do something, I know I can count on him. How many people do you know who are that reliable?"

A Christian you can count on

Look It Up: People respect and seek out people characterized by dependability. The Apostle Paul had some dependable friends—the married couple Priscilla and Aquila. Tentmakers by trade, they began to work with Paul in Corinth. As Paul saw how reliable they were, he began to count on them more and more for help in his missionary ventures (Acts 18:18-26).

They were so dependable that when Paul wrote the church in Rome he included this greeting: "Greet Priscilla and Aquila, my fellow workers in Christ Jesus. They risked their lives for me" (Romans 16:3-4).

Think It Through: Suppose you've commited yourself to being at a meeting when a friend calls to say he has tickets to see your favorite group in concert that same evening. Or what if you agree to go out with someone, and later a better opportunity arises for you to go out with someone else?

Dependability carries a high price tag. It means that we keep our word no matter what—even if we have to make some unexpected sacrifices.

Work It Out: Here's an assignment that will help you be the kind of person that people can count on.

Ask (make) your best friend tell you truthfully whether or not you're a dependable person. If the answer is not what you want to hear, don't attack your friend! Attack the problem.

Begin keeping a schedule book so that you can fulfill all your obligations. Don't commit to more than you can handle. Finally, ask God to make you more reliable.

Nail It Down: Meditate on Psalm 15:1-5. This weekend read about one dependable lady—Ruth. Read Ruth 1 on Saturday and reread the same chapter on Sunday.

❖❖❖❖❖❖❖❖❖ FIVE CHARACTER

~~~~~ GOD'S WILL ~~~~~~~~~
The Father's Requirements

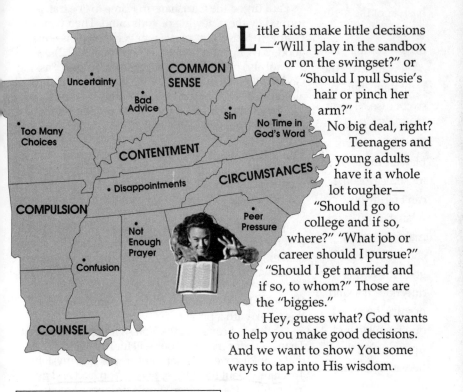

Uncertainty

COMMON
SENSE

Bad
Advice

Sin

No Time in
God's Word

Too Many
Choices

CONTENTMENT

CIRCUMSTANCES

• Disappointments

COMPULSION

Peer
Pressure

Not
Enough
Prayer

Confusion

COUNSEL

L ittle kids make little decisions —"Will I play in the sandbox or on the swingset?" or "Should I pull Susie's hair or pinch her arm?"

No big deal, right? Teenagers and young adults have it a whole lot tougher— "Should I go to college and if so, where?" "What job or career should I pursue?" "Should I get married and if so, to whom?" Those are the "biggies."

Hey, guess what? God wants to help you make good decisions. And we want to show You some ways to tap into His wisdom.

The Key to God's Will

★	— God's Word	
• Confusion	— Obstacles	
-----------	— Biblical Boundaries	
COUNSEL	— C's of Choosing	

| 0 | God's Time Line | 100 |

★ *"I will instruct you and teach you in the way you should go, I will counsel you and watch over you" (Psalm 32:8).*

~~~~~~~~~~~~~~~~~~~~~~~~~~~~~~~~~~~~

Can you relate to this?

Grant is facing some big decisions —where to go to college, what to major in, if he and Susan have any sort of future—and he hasn't got the foggiest idea of what to do. He complains:

"I want to do the right thing, but I'm so confused. I mean, I know God must have some sort of plan for my life, but for some reason, I can't figure out what it is. What if I make the wrong choices? What if I go in the wrong direction? It's kind of scary, because I don't want to end up regretting the decisions I make."

The mystery is history

Look It Up: There's no need to freak out over the What-should-I-do-type questions. Discovering God's will for your life is not like searching for buried treasure in the ocean. His will can be known.

Paul urged the Christians in Rome to "be transformed by the renewing of your mind. Then you will be able to test and approve what God's will is—his good, pleasing and perfect will" (Romans 12:2).

Paul also prayed for the believers in Colosse, "asking God to fill [them] with the knowledge of his will through all spiritual wisdom and understanding" (Colossians 1:9).

Obviously, Paul thought it was possible—and essential—to know God's will.

Think It Through: Most parents are always giving their kids advice, telling them, "You need to do this" or "If I were in your shoes, I'd do that." Why? Usually because they love their kids and don't want them to make wrong choices.

In a much greater way God loves us and wants the best for us. Why then do we often think that He sits in heaven, tight-lipped and unwilling to give us guidance when we need it?

Work It Out: Why not start off your study of God's will this week with a prayer:

"Father in heaven, thank You so much for loving me. Thank You for making Your will for my life something that I can discover and not some impossible mystery. Teach me about the different ways You lead and guide Your children as I look at Your Word the next few days. You know I want my life to count for You. You know I want to do Your will. Help me through Christ. Amen."

Nail It Down: Read Psalm 143:10.

〜〜〜〜〜〜〜 ONE **GOD'S WILL** 〜

As soon as sixteen-year-old Shelly graduates next May, she intends to marry her boyfriend Will, who's 19.

She's got it all planned. He'll keep working at his construction job. She'll enroll in beauty school. And they'll live happily ever after.

There's one major problem. Shelly is a Christian and Will isn't. She argues, "But you don't really know Will. He's so sweet! And he promises that he'll come to church with me. I just know this is God's will. We really love each other. He'll become a Christian later."

Why ask when He's answered?

Look It Up: So much of God's will for our lives is already revealed—spelled out in the pages of the Bible.

• "God our Savior . . . wants all men to be saved and to come to a knowledge of the truth" (1 Timothy 2:3-4).

• "It is God's will that you should be sanctified: that you should avoid sexual immorality" (1 Thessalonians 4:3).

• "Be joyful always; pray continually; give thanks in all circumstances, for this is God's will for you in Christ Jesus" (1 Thessalonians 5:16-18).

Think It Through: By carefully studying the commands and principles of God's Word, we can come up with a list of things which are clearly God's will for our lives. We might not find answers to specific questions like, "Which school should I attend?", but we can discover a lot of good, basic guidelines.

Should a Christian ever pray about whether God wants him to rob a bank? Why not? Based on 2 Corinthians 6:14-18, what is God's will for Shelly?

Work It Out: Quickly read through Romans 12:9-21. Underline with pencil the commands in this passage.

These are not suggestions that you can take or leave. These requirements are the will of God for your life.

Determine that you will live according to these verses today and every day. If we don't follow the parts of God's will that He has already revealed to us in His Word, why should He give us special guidance in other areas of life?

Nail It Down: See more of God's will for your life in Ephesians 5.

Pray About It:

TWO

165

A group of Blaine's friends from Southside High are taking a senior trip to Florida. Blaine's pretty sure it's going to be a wild trip—in fact by the end of the week, almost the whole graduating class will be there. A couple of the guys going are Christian friends from church, but most of them aren't.

Blaine feels torn. He wants to be with his friends. But at the same time, he doesn't want to go down there, get in a bunch of tempting situations, and blow his witness.

How can he figure out what's best?

Getting guidance from God

Look It Up: Christians often overlook one of the best ways to discover God's will—simply talking to God in prayer.

When the Israelites entered Canaan, they were commanded to defeat and destroy all the inhabitants of the land. After a couple of victories, they encountered a group of people from nearby Gibeon who pretended to be from a faraway land. The Gibeonites' deception worked perfectly because "the men of Israel . . . did not inquire of the LORD. Then Joshua made a treaty of peace with [the Gibeonites] to let them live" (Joshua 9:14-15).

The point is this: by not seeking God's wisdom in complicated situations, we're asking for trouble.

Think It Through: Many thousands of people write to Ann Landers and Dear Abby for advice. Often the counsel they get is superficial. Why do so many Christians fail to ask God for help in making decisions?

Do you think Christians may not talk to God about what to do because deep down they already know what's best? Is it possible Blaine feels this way?

Work It Out: If you're facing a tough decision, you can't afford not to get God's wisdom. You need to talk things over with Him . . . right now.

Like many things in the Christian faith, prayer is a mystery. But that doesn't mean it's impossible. God talks to us in His Word and world. He's designed prayer as the way we talk to Him.

Present your situation to Him, and ask Him to reveal the best thing to do. Sooner or later, you'll get the answer you need (maybe not what you want, and maybe not the way you expect, but definitely what you need).

Nail It Down: Read Philippians 4:6-7.

THREE GOD'S WILL

Jill has basically two goals in life: to develop her God-given artistic abilities and to reach people for Christ. Now, however, she's being forced to choose between two good opportunities.

She's been offered a job at one of the leading art galleries in her city—a chance to learn new things and meet some talented, influential people. She's also just been given the opportunity to travel with a missionary team to Mexico. She'd love to do both, but if she goes to Mexico for three weeks, someone else will get the job in the gallery.

Jill has three days to decide!

"C's" for charting your course

Look It Up: Choosing between several good options is extremely tough. But you can discover the best option by evaluating these two C's:

• Circumstances. Realize that there are no coincidences. God is in control of our lives and uses every incident to direct our steps. Investigate the various circumstances—spiritual, financial, emotional, social, physical—surrounding each option before deciding.

• Counsel. Don't neglect the wisdom of older, more mature Christians—your parents, pastor, teachers, youth workers. "Plans fail for lack of counsel, but with many advisers they succeed" (Proverbs 15:22).

Think It Through: If your goal is to be a great drummer, but you have neither rhythm nor a drumset, your circumstances might be God's way of telling you that He has something else for you. If your minister keeps telling you, "God has given you some real gifts." Maybe God is using such counsel to guide you.

But be careful! Circumstances can also make wrong choices look good. And some counsel, though meant for good, can be totally off base. Use these C's cautiously and only after much prayer.

Work It Out: On an index card, write down some tough choices you face today as well as "biggies" that loom on the horizon. Then take all the aspects of knowing God's will we've talked about so far and see if you can summarize them on another index card. The point is to develop a simple tool that you can carry around with you to help you make good decisions in tough situations.

If you're still unsure about which way to go, there are a few more tips tomorrow. Hang on.

Nail It Down: Read Exodus 18:13-27.

Pray About It:

F O U R

167

Stan has been accepted at two different schools—Freedom University and Einstein College. He has good friends going to each place. He likes certain things about each school. What should he do?

• Should Angela take a job at the clothing store or the dry-cleaners? The pay is about the same.

• Curt can either play baseball or be in the spring play, but not both. He's both a good athlete and a gifted actor.

Inner C's for inner peace

Look It Up: Here are three more C's to find God's will:

1. Common Sense. Christianity is a rational faith. God is a logical God. We're to love Him with our minds, using our biblically informed reason in decision-making. Paul often used common sense (Acts 15:38).

2. Compulsion. Often God gives us inner impressions to follow or not to follow a certain course. This was Paul's experience: "And now, compelled by the Spirit, I am going to Jerusalem" (Acts 20:22). Such leading is for us as well. "Those who are led by the Spirit of God are sons of God" (Romans 8:14). Remember, if you feel led, it's probably God. If you feel pressured, it's probably not.

3. Contentment. Being in God's will should result in an inner peace in our lives (Colossians 3:15).

Think It Through: In light of the following facts, what would your counsel be? Stan found out that he doesn't have the money for Einstein College. Plus it doesn't offer the major he wants. Angela has been praying a lot and has a gut feeling that she ought to work at the clothing store. Curt, even though he's a good actor, doesn't enjoy drama nearly as much as baseball.

Again, be careful not to make decisions solely on these factors. Sometimes God asks His people to do things that seem illogical (Hosea 3:1). Sometimes inner impressions can mislead us. Sometimes His will isn't pleasant (Jonah 1:1-2). Always evaluate these C's in light of His Word.

Work It Out: Because we've barely scratched the surface of figuring out what the Father wants, ask your youth pastor to recommend a book on knowing God's will.

Meanwhile, make sure you begin putting these introductory suggestions into practice. Start today.

Nail It Down: Read Ephesians 5:17. Use your devotional times this weekend to memorize this short verse.

FIVE GOD'S WILL

FAMILY
The Tuckers' Trip

There are two types of teenagers in the world: those who are satisfied with their home life, and those who aren't. This is a week for those in the second category.

For some good ideas on where to begin to make your family situation better, jump in the car with the Tuckers for a trip to Aunt Martha's. It won't be like a trip to Disney World, but the memories will last a whole lot longer.

"Dear children, let us not love with words or tongue but with actions and in truth" (1 John 3:18).

Mr. Tucker is watching the news. Mrs. Tucker is making Spam casserole. Teresa, 16, is doing homework. Troy, 13, is in his room listening to a tape by the rock group Lust Mongrel. Tad, 3, is spraying the cat with Windex.

Later, as the Tuckers sit down to eat, the phone rings. Bad news—Aunt Martha is in a hospital in Des Moines, and she's not doing well. Mr. Tucker hangs up the phone, confers with Mrs. Tucker, and delivers the decision: The whole family will leave for Iowa in the morning.

So much for Teresa's and Troy's weekend plans.

Subordination, not argumentation

Look It Up: When parents make decisions under pressure without consulting their kids, they're not trying to be unfair or insensitive. Generally speaking, they're just trying to choose the best overall plan for everyone.

In such cases, it's wise to remember two verses from God's Word:
• "Do everything without complaining or arguing" (Philippians 2:14).
• "A gentle answer turns away wrath, but a harsh word stirs up anger. The tongue of the wise commends knowledge, but the mouth of the fool gushes folly" (Proverbs 15:1-2).

Think It Through: Think back to a time when you were in a situation similar to Teresa's or Troy's. How did you react? What happened as a result? Is there anything you could have done, or not done, to have improved the situation?

Work It Out: When a parental decision torpedoes your plans, you can either (a) explode in anger and begin a huge argument (which not only goes against God's Word, but also makes your parents furious) or (b) say nothing at first, choosing instead to chill out for a while.

Obviously, "b" is the wiser choice. After you've relaxed, ask your parents if you can talk with them for a few minutes. Start off by saying, "Mom, Dad, I'm willing to do whatever you want, but I had sort of been planning on _____. It's really important to me. Can we talk about it?"

When you state your thoughts and feelings in a calm, gentle manner, you stand a much better chance of being heard—and you create a lot less friction.

Nail It Down: Read Ephesians 6:1-3.

⊃OOOOOOOOOO ◯◯ **ONE FAMILY** OOOOO ◯◯◯◯◯

Troy raised quite a ruckus about going to Aunt Martha's and was ordered from the table—no more Spam for him!

Teresa waited and talked with her parents later in the evening. She told them about the big weekend ski party and why it was important to her. "Plus," she added, "If I went, I'd just end up sitting around."

Her parents listened carefully. When she finished, her mom said, "Teresa, I know your plans are important, really I do. But Aunt Martha needs me, and I need you to help with Tad. I need you to come with us."

Consideration, not manipulation

Look It Up: Have you ever stopped to think that sometimes your parents really need you? It's true. They're not emotionally invincible. They have feelings and hurts and fears too. And when those times come, you need to lay aside your own plans and think of them first.

"Be devoted to one another in brotherly love. Honor one another above yourselves" (Romans 12:10).

"A new command I give you: Love one another. As I have loved you, so you must love one another" (John 13:34).

Think It Through: Consider that last verse. It's a statement by Jesus. He tells us to love one other the same way He loved us (that even includes parents).

What does that mean? When we needed forgiveness because of our sins, Jesus didn't remain in heaven and say, "I love you down there and hope you get your problems worked out." No! His love motivated Him to action. He made a huge sacrifice—His life—for us. In the same way, when our parents are depending on us, we need to be willing to make the necessary sacrifices.

How would you react in Teresa's situation?

Work It Out: Maybe your parents are down because of problems in the family or difficulties at work. If so, do something today to support them emotionally and spiritually. Give them a big hug, sit down and talk to them, offer to do some extra jobs, pray for them.

And next time they do request your help, blow their minds by being agreeable and not rocking the boat. (This is one guaranteed way to improve things at your house—no kidding!)

Nail It Down: Read 1 Thessalonians 4:9-10.

Pray About It:

OOOOOOO

T W O

171

It's your basic traveling nightmare.

Mr. Tucker is complaining because the windshield wipers aren't working. Mrs. Tucker is trying to clean up Tad's spilled milkshake. Troy is upset about his broken Walkman and telling Teresa to move her "big fat legs."

What about Teresa? She feels like doing all of the following: screaming; heaving Troy out the window; giving knock-out drops to Tad; and telling her dad to get off at the next exit, drop her off at a luxurious hotel with the credit card, and pick her up on the way back home.

Affirmation not agitation

Look It Up: It's not just during trips that families get on each others' nerves. Patience can wear thin anytime. But before you snap, remember these verses:

• "Be completely humble and gentle; be patient, bearing with one another in love" (Ephesians 4:2).

• "Live in peace with each other. And we urge you . . . help the weak, be patient with everyone. Make sure that nobody pays back wrong for wrong, but always try to be kind to each other" (1 Thessalonians 5:13-15).

• "Therefore, as God's chosen people, holy and dearly loved, clothe yourselves with compassion, kindness, humility, gentleness and patience" (Colossians 3:12).

Think It Through: So many times we feel like letting our brothers or sisters have it. Or we feel like telling off our parents. And yet, we're not to live by our feelings. Christians are to live by faith in God's Word.

What if Teresa, instead of acting on her feelings, responded to her situation by faithfully obeying God's Word? What if she offered to let Troy use her Walkman? What if she cleaned up Tad's mess and then played with him? Could such actions help change the mood in the Tucker car?

Work It Out: Chances are, someone in your family, at some time today, will be in a bad mood. How should you respond?

• Be patient—Ask God's Spirit to control your attitudes and tongue to keep you from saying or doing things that are antagonistic.

• Be kind—Come up with a creative way to help ease the situation. Then jump in and share the family member's burden.

Nail It Down: Read Galatians 5:22-23.

∞∞∞∞∞∞∞ THREE **FAMILY** ∞∞∞∞∞∞∞∞∞

172

When the
Tuckers got
to Aunt Martha's,
Teresa surveyed
the situation and
whispered to Troy,
"This isn't going to
be fun. She doesn't
have a TV or VCR,
and there isn't a
mall within 20
miles."

"I know," he
replied. "It's a
prison."

Later that day
they discovered the
attic . . . all kinds of
old stuff—trunks
full of old family
pictures, letters,
mementos, a huge
stamp collection,
and an old family
tree, listing most of
their ancestors.

Suddenly Teresa
and Troy were hav-
ing fun talking to
each other . . . and
to their parents in
the evenings.

Communication not alienation

Look It Up: These days, few families spend much time actually talking with and listening to each other. That's sad!

While we can't really point to a verse that says, "Spend time on a regular basis talking to your family," we can see that all the way through the Bible this kind of communication is important. Men and women of God gathered with their relatives and friends to discuss God and life (for one of many examples of this principle at work, see Acts 2).

Take note of this verse too: "Pleasant words are a honeycomb, sweet to the soul and healing to the bones" (Proverbs 16:24).

Think It Through: How come it's so easy to get into an argument with another family member and so hard to have a meaningful conversation? How long has it been since you sat down with a parent or a brother or sister and said, "So tell me, how are things with you?"

If you want to improve your home situation, there's no better way to start than to begin communicating.

Work It Out: You don't have to be stranded at your Aunt Martha's in order to have decent conversations with the other members of your family. Good communication can happen anywhere, anytime, if you make it a priority.

Tell your parents you want to have a family forum once a month just to talk about things. Then sit back and let the questions fly. You'll be amazed to hear how your parents met each other, what life was like for them growing up, and what their views are on all the hot issues. Have each person share personal complaints, and suggest ways to improve the family situation.

Nail It Down: Read Proverbs 18:21.

Pray About It:

OOOOOOO FOUR

By the third day, Aunt Martha was doing much better. The Tuckers figured that she'd eventually have to be put in a convalescent home, probably in their hometown. They agreed that Mrs. Tucker would fly back in two weeks to make the arrangements.

That evening Mr. Tucker suddenly said, "Hey, I've got an idea. Let's go celebrate. Yesterday I saw one of those Japanese restaurants where they cook at your table. And it was in a big mall with a movie theater. Anybody ready for a good time?"

Appreciation not deterioration

Look It Up: Your parents aren't perfect, and they can't give you everything. But they generally try to make your situation better. How you respond to their efforts is important.

As a Christian, you are expected to show appreciation to people who have shown kindness to you.

• Example # 1—Old Testament Boaz: " 'The LORD bless you, my daughter,' he replied. 'This kindness is greater than that which you showed earlier' " (Ruth 3:10).

• Example #2—New Testament Paul: "Priscilla and Aquila . . . risked their lives for me. Not only I but all the churches of the Gentiles are grateful to them" (Romans 16:3-4).

Think It Through: How do you feel when you do something nice for someone, and he or she doesn't show any appreciation?

What if Teresa and Troy had rolled their eyes and made some kind of remark like, "Sure, Dad, you'll probably want us all to go see 'The Little Mermaid.' "

Work It Out: Statistics show that the average parents spend more than $100,000 to raise each one of their children. That's some serious cash! When was the last time you thanked your folks for all their sacrifices for you?

They don't have to: let you use the car, buy you new jeans, send you to camp, pay for your braces, give you an allowance, or do a lot of the other things.

Write them a note of appreciation. Or better yet, give them a big hug today and tell them face to face how grateful you are for their love.

Nail It Down: Read Colossians 3:15. On both Saturday and Sunday read Paul's classic family instructions: Ephesians 5:22-6:4.

◗◯◯◯◯◯◯◯◯◯ F I V E **FAMILY** ◯◯◯◯◯◯◯◯◯◯◯